LEARN TO Sew
and Embroider

LEARN TO Sew
and Embroider

35 projects using simple stitches, cute embroidery, and pretty appliqué

Emma Hardy

CICO **kidz**

This edition published in 2023 by CICO Kidz

An imprint of Ryland Peters & Small

341 E 116th St
New York, NY 10029

20–21 Jockey's Fields
London WC1R 4BW

www.rylandpeters.com

10 9 8 7 6 5 4 3 2 1

First published in 2016 as My First
Stitching & Sewing Book

Text © Emma Hardy 2016
Design, photography, and illustration
© CICO Kidz 2016

A CIP catalog record for this book is
available from the Library of Congress
and the British Library.

ISBN: 978-1-80065-201-9

Printed in China

Editor: Sarah Hoggett
Designer: Barbara Zuniga
Photographer: Debbie Patterson
Illustrator: Rachel Boulton
Character illustrations: Hannah George
Template illustrations: Stephen Dew
Stylist: Emma Hardy

Art director: Sally Powell
Production manager: Gordana Simakovic
Publishing manager: Penny Craig
Publisher: Cindy Richards

MIX
Paper | Supporting
responsible forestry
FSC® C008047

Contents

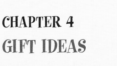

Introduction

Being able to sew is a really great skill to have—and as you'll see from this book, it's easier than you might think. You don't even need much equipment to get started. However, it is a good idea to put together a sewing box so that you will have all the tools you need to hand; you can buy one from a fabric store or just use an old tin or box that you have already. You don't need large pieces of fabric for any of the projects in this book, so you may be able to re-use scraps left over from other projects or visit your local fabric store and look for offcuts and remnants, which are often quite cheap.

In this book, there are four chapters—Jewelry and Accessories, Toys and Dolls, Stationery and Decorations, and Gift Ideas. Each project has a materials and tools list to show you what you will need, and then simple step-by-step instructions to guide you through. There is also a techniques section to help you learn all the basic stitches and skills.

Once you've mastered the basics, there'll be no stopping you! You'll be able to make lots of fun and original projects for yourself and your friends and family. From fruit brooches, a cute sock dog, and handy felt stationery pots to a stylish apron and pretty bunting, this book is packed with ideas to inspire you.

Project levels

Level 1
These projects are all quick and very easy. They require only simple cutting out and stitching.

Level 2
These projects are a little more difficult and may take a bit longer or use some slightly harder stitches.

Level 3
These are more ambitious projects that often need you to sew longer seams and careful small stitches to make them strong. Some also need you to ask an adult's help to use an iron.

Your sewing box

We suggest you put together a sewing box that contains:

A pencil

A pen

A ruler

A tape measure

Squared paper (e.g. from a math book) for making patterns

Plain paper for tracing templates

Scissors for cutting paper

Sharp scissors kept especially for cutting fabric

Pins

Needles, including some big ones with big eyes

A needle threader (this will save you a lot of time!)

Cotton thread, embroidery floss (thread), and yarn (wool) in different colors

Polyester toy stuffing

Glue

Pinking shears

Dressmaker's chalk

You also need to start a collection of different materials, so look out for:

Buttons—especially pretty ones. Cut them off clothes that are too worn out to pass on, or look out for boxes of them in thrift stores (charity shops) and garage sales.

Ribbons and braids—look out for them on gifts or on boxes of chocolates. They will always come in useful.

Fabrics—some you will have to buy, but often, small leftover pieces (remnants) are sold very cheaply. A collection of different-colored felts is a must and you can buy these at craft stores or online. Remember to save pieces of fabric from clothes that are too worn out to pass on, and to keep leftover scraps from other projects. Ask any adult stitchers you know to keep any leftover fabric for you. They are sure to want to encourage a new stitcher!

Sewing Techniques

The best way to learn something new is to start from the beginning. Read this section on basic techniques and sewing skills carefully—you will need to know how to use a pattern, how to thread a needle, and how to sew on a button. Here you will also find instructions for the special stitches and decorative touches that will make your projects unique.

Using a pattern

There are lots of templates in this book to help you make patterns for the projects. To use them:

1 Trace the template onto tracing paper or thin paper that you can see through, and cut them out to make a pattern.

2 Pin this pattern onto your fabric, making sure that the fabric is flat with no creases. Position the pattern close to the edges of the fabric so that you don't waste any. Try to pin patterns, especially rectangles, in line with the tiny threads you can see in the fabric (on felt it doesn't matter). If you need two pieces that are the same shape, fold the fabric over and pin the pattern so the pins go through both layers.

How to use half-size or quarter-size templates

Some of the templates (on pages 122–27) need to be doubled or quadrupled in size to make the pattern large enough. Ask somebody to photocopy the template for you, using the 200% zoom button on the photocopier to double a template in size. For quarter-size templates, double in size (200% zoom), then double again (another 200%).

3 If the pattern has a dotted fold line on it, fold the fabric over and pin the pattern piece onto it, positioning the fold line on the pattern along the fold of the fabric. Cut around the pattern as close to the edge as you can.

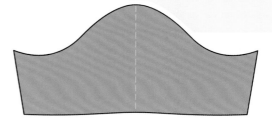

4 Remove the pins and the pattern. When the shape is opened out, it will be doubled.

Square or rectangular templates

• Many of the projects start with a square or rectangular pattern. To cut these out, make a paper pattern first.

• For small squares and rectangles, it is easiest to draw these on squared paper—that way, you can be sure that all your angles are right angles.

• For large squares that won't fit on the squared paper, mark the length of the sides on a corner of a large sheet of newspaper or brown wrapping paper. Join up the two marks to make a triangle. Fold the triangle over along this line and cut around it; that will give you a perfect square.

• For large rectangles, you will need to use a set square to draw the right angles. Carefully check the lengths of each side when you have drawn them to make sure that opposite sides are equal.

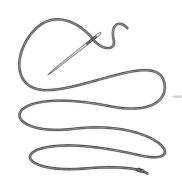

Threading a needle

You won't be able to start sewing without threading your needle!

1 Thread your needle with about 25 in. (65 cm) of thread or yarn (wool). Pull about 6 in. (15 cm) of the thread through the needle. Tie two knots on top of each other at the other end.

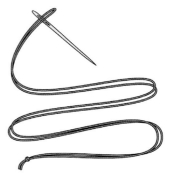

 2 For a double thread, which is stronger, pull the thread through the needle until the thread is doubled over and tie a knot in the two ends together.

Running stitch

This is the simplest stitch and can be used in embroidery and for joining two layers of fabric together. It is very easy to do, but not very strong. Secure the end of the thread with a few small stitches. Push the needle down through the fabric a little way along, then bring it back up through the fabric a little further along. Repeat to form a row of stitches.

Backstitch

This is a very useful stitch, since it is strong and similar to the stitches used on a sewing machine. It makes a solid line of stitches.

1 Start as if you were sewing running stitch. Sew one stitch and bring the needle back up to start the second stitch.

2 This time, instead of going forward, go back and push the needle through at the end of your first stitch.

3 Bring it out again a stitch length past the thread. Keep going to make an even line of stitches with no gaps.

French knot

French knots are useful for sewing tiny eyes and the centers of flowers. They are a bit tricky, so practice on some scrap material first.

1 Knot your thread and bring the needle up from the back of the fabric to the front. Wrap the thread once or twice around the tip of the needle, then push the needle back in, right next to the place it came up.

2 As you push the needle in with one hand, hold the wrapped-around threads tightly against the fabric with the thumbnail of your other hand. Pull the needle all the way through. The wraps will form a knot on the surface of the fabric.

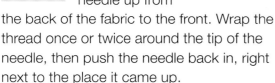

Whipstitch

This stitch is used to sew two layers of fabric together with stitches that show at the edges. It is also useful to close up a gap after stuffing an object.

Begin with a knot or a few small stitches at the back of the two layers. Push the needle through both layers to the front, ⅛ in. (2–3 mm) from the edge, and pull the thread right through. Take the needle over the top of both layers to the back again and push it through to the front a little way along the seam. The stitches go over and over the edges of the two fabrics. Finish with a knot or a few small stitches.

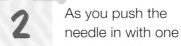

Blanket stitch

1 Bring the needle through at the edge of the fabric.

2 Push the needle back through the fabric a short distance from the edge and loop the thread under the needle. Pull the needle and thread as far as you can to make the first stitch.

3 Make another stitch to the right of this and again loop the thread under the needle. Continue along the fabric and finish with a few small stitches or a knot on the underside.

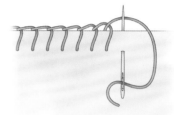

Sewing on a button

You can use buttons as decorations—and you never know when you'll need to sew a button onto some clothes!

1 Mark the place where you want the button to go. Push the needle up from the back of the fabric and sew a few stitches over and over in this place.

2 Now bring the needle up through one of the holes in the button. Push the needle back down through the second hole and through the fabric. Bring it back up through the first hole. Repeat this five or six times. If there are four holes in the button, use all four of them to make a cross pattern. Make sure you keep the stitches close together under the middle of the button.

3 Finish with a few small stitches over and over on the back of the fabric and trim the thread.

Pressing seams open

Often when you have stitched a seam, you will need to press it open.

Ask an adult to help you do this. Run the tip of the iron along the seam so the two edges of fabric open up to lie flat on either side of the seam.

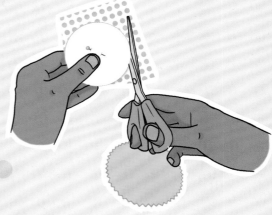

chapter 1
Jewelry and Accessories

Raccoon Scarf

😊 😊 ⚪

This is a scarf that will keep you warm and make everyone smile! What's more, it's simple to make—you just need to use running stitch and whipstitch, two of the easiest stitches to sew.

You will need

Paper for templates

Templates on page 122

16 x 45 in. (40 x 115 cm) pale gray fleece

10 x 13 in. (25 x 35 cm) black fleece

5 x 7 in. (13 x 18 cm) cream fleece

2 black buttons, approx. ½ in. (12 mm) in diameter, for eyes

Black and cream embroidery floss (thread)

White sewing thread

Pencil and ruler

Scissors

Sticky tape

Pins

Embroidery and sewing needles

1 On the paper, draw a long rectangle measuring 24 x 6 in. (60 x 15 cm) and cut it out. Enlarge the templates on page 122 by 200% and cut them out. Tape the head and tail paper templates to the ends of the paper rectangle to make the raccoon pattern. Fold the gray fleece in half, pin the raccoon pattern to it, and cut it out carefully to give you two scarf pieces.

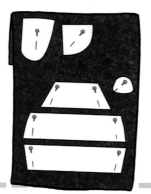

2 Using the templates, cut out the outer eyes, ears, nose, and the three stripes for the tail from black fleece. You'll need to cut two outer eyes and two outer ears, so fold the short end of the fleece over so that it's doubled—then you can cut both eyes and ears at the same time. Then cut out the inner eyes, inner ears, and face from cream fleece; again, fold the short end of the fleece over so that you can cut two inner eyes and ears at the same time.

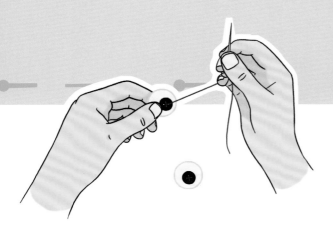

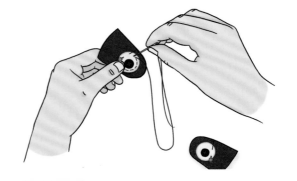

3 Thread an embroidery needle with black embroidery floss (thread) and tie a knot in the end. Sew one black button onto each of the cream inner eyes (see page 11).

4 Pin the cream inner eyes onto the black outer eyes. Still using black floss, sew them in place with running stitch (see page 9), starting and finishing with a knot on the wrong side.

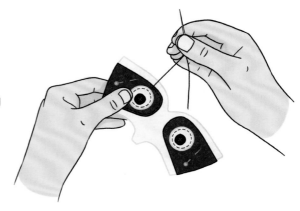

5 Pin the black outer eyes onto the cream fleece face piece, matching up the outer edges. Sew around the curved edge on both eyes with running stitch, as before.

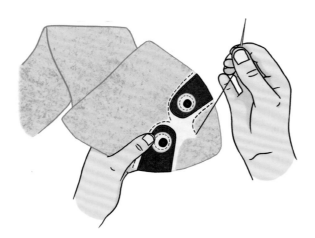

6 Pin the cream face piece to the right side of one of the gray fleece scarf pieces. Using black embroidery floss, sew along the top and bottom edges with running stitch, as before.

7 Using running stitch, sew the cream inner ears to the black outer ears, then pin and stitch them above the face onto the scarf. Then stitch the black nose in place.

8 Thread your needle with cream embroidery floss. Pin the stripes to the right side of the tail end of the scarf and stitch across the top and bottom edges with running stitch.

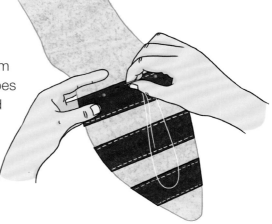

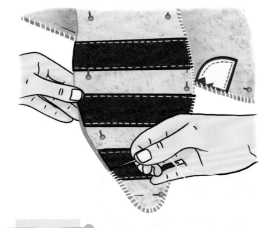

9 Lay the second gray scarf piece on the table, right side down, and place the top piece right side up on top of it, matching up all the edges. Pin the two layers together all the way around. Thread a needle with white sewing thread and whipstitch (see page 10) all the way around, starting and finishing with a few small stitches.

Embroidered Buttons

Jazz up a plain bag with a scattering of these pretty buttons. Self-cover buttons can be bought from haberdashery stores, but try to buy plastic rather than metal ones as they are easier to use. You can make several buttons from one square of fabric, but they look more fun in different colors.

You will need

9-in. (23-cm) squares of plain fabric (I used four different colors; one square is enough to make several buttons)

Plastic self-cover buttons in different sizes (mine ranged from ¾ to 1½ in./20 to 38 mm)

Embroidery flosses (threads) in pretty pastel colors

5-in. (13-cm) or larger embroidery hoop

Pencil

Tailor's chalk

Embroidery needle

Scissors

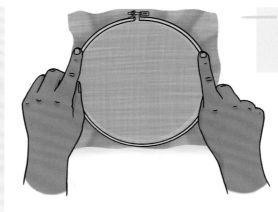

1 Undo the screw on the embroidery hoop and separate the inner and outer rings. Place one square of fabric over the inner hoop. Place the outer hoop on top and tighten the screw, gently pulling the fabric so that it is tight.

2 On the packet of self-cover buttons, there will be a template for the size of button that you are using. Cut this out, hold it on the fabric in your hoop, and draw around it in pencil. This circle is much bigger than the button, because you need to leave a border of fabric around your stitching to fold around the button.

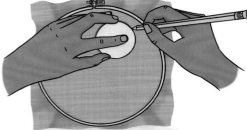

Tip
Don't put the template right in the middle of the hoop. If you put it nearer the edge, you'll be able to get several buttons out of one piece of fabric.

3 Thread the needle with embroidery floss (thread) in a color that contrasts with the fabric , and tie a knot in the end. Bring the needle up through the fabric from the underside to the front. Decide on the pattern that you would like to sew and follow the instructions opposite.

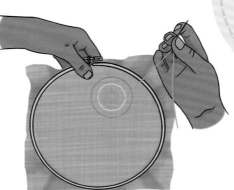

Embroidering the buttons

Be sure not to embroider right up to the edge of the circle—you need to leave space all around for when you fold the fabric over the button. To help you know where to stitch, place the button upside down in the middle of the circle and draw around it in tailor's chalk, which will rub off later.

For a dotty button
Make French knots (see page 10) randomly inside the chalk circle. Finish with a knot on the underside of the fabric.

For a spiral
Make backstitches (see page 10) in a spiral shape, keeping inside the chalk circle. Don't worry too much about it being neat—it will look lovely when fixed onto the button! Again, make sure that you do not go over where the button will be. Finish on the underside with a knot.

For a star or flower shape
Make four large stitches crossing over each other, or seven small stitches starting from the center and working outward.

For a sprinkles pattern
Sew small stitches randomly all over the center, inside the chalk circle.

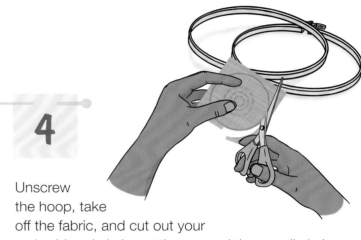

4

Unscrew the hoop, take off the fabric, and cut out your embroidered circle, cutting around the pencil circle you drew in step 2. It doesn't matter if your cutting is a bit wobbly and it isn't a perfect circle, so long as you've left enough space all around the stitching to fold the fabric over the button.

5 Following the button manufacturer's instructions, separate the button into its two pieces. Be careful of the teeth inside the front of the button—they need to be sharp to hold the fabric firmly. Place the button front on the back of the embroidered circle, making sure that it fits neatly and the embroidery is in the middle. Fold the fabric around the button, stretching it tight and pushing it down over the teeth on the back. Press on the button back so that the two halves snap together. When you have made several buttons, stitch them onto a plain bag or purse (see page 11) to make a pretty decoration.

Felt and Ribbon Bracelet

Jazz up your jewelry box with these pretty flower bracelets. Make daisies from white and yellow felt or choose bright colors for a lovely summery look. Stitch the flowers onto gingham ribbon and simply tie the bracelets around your wrist to add the finishing touch to your outfit.

You will need

Templates on page 123

Three 2½-in. (6-cm) pieces of felt if you are using three different colors, or one 2½ x 8-in. (6 x 20-cm) piece if you want all the flowers to be the same color

2½ x 6 in. (6 x 15 cm) green felt

18 in. (45 cm) gingham ribbon, ⅜ in. (1 cm) wide

Three buttons, ½ in. (12 mm) in diameter

White sewing thread

Paper

Pencil

Marker pen

Scissors

Pins

Sewing needle

1 Photocopy the templates on page 123 or trace them onto scrap paper, and cut them out.

2 Pin the paper flower to a piece of felt, draw around it carefully with a marker pen, then take off the pattern and pins. Cut it out carefully. Do this twice more, so that you have three felt flowers altogether.

3 Pin the paper leaf to the green felt, draw around it, then take off the pattern and pins. Cut it out carefully. Do this two more times, so that you have three felt leaves altogether.

A bright **BUTTON** bracelet

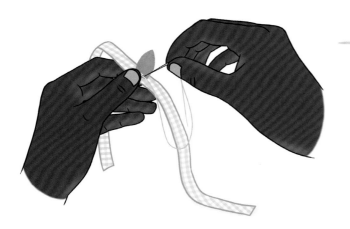

4 Thread your needle with white sewing thread. Find the middle of the ribbon and make a few small stitches. Bring the needle up through the bottom of a felt leaf (turn it over first if you can see any pen marks) and back down through both the leaf and the ribbon. Do this three or four times to fix the leaf securely to the ribbon.

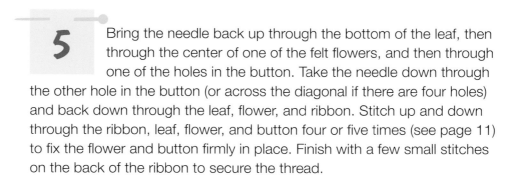

5 Bring the needle back up through the bottom of the leaf, then through the center of one of the felt flowers, and then through one of the holes in the button. Take the needle down through the other hole in the button (or across the diagonal if there are four holes) and back down through the leaf, flower, and ribbon. Stitch up and down through the ribbon, leaf, flower, and button four or five times (see page 11) to fix the flower and button firmly in place. Finish with a few small stitches on the back of the ribbon to secure the thread.

6 Stitch the other two leaves, flowers, and buttons onto the ribbon about ⅜ in. (1 cm) either side of the first flower.

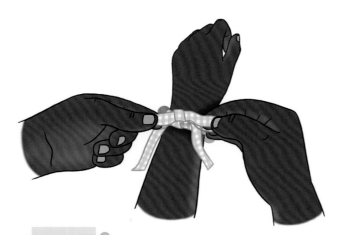

7 To finish, ask one of your family to tie it around your wrist in a neat bow, or tie it around a friend's wrist as a lovely gift.

Flower Shoe Decorations

Need to brighten up a boring pair of sneakers?
Making pretty fabric flowers is easy to do and will
create a really original look that will definitely get you noticed!
This project is a great way of using up scraps of fabric left over from
making other things, so it won't cost you a cent either.

You will need

Template on page 123

6 x 12 in. (15 x 30 cm) each of
two fabrics

3 x 10 in. (8 x 26 cm) green felt

Four buttons, ⅝ in. (1.5 cm)
in diameter

Plain shoes or sneakers

White sewing thread

Paper

Pencil

Ruler

Pins

Scissors

Sewing needle

Fabric glue

1 Take your ruler and go find a small bowl, cup, or glass that is about 3 in. (8 cm) in diameter. Draw around it on paper and cut out the circle for a template.

2 Fold a piece of fabric in half and pin the paper circle to it. Cut the circle out. Don't worry too much about being very neat, as the edges will not show. Do the same thing with the second fabric. You will now have four circles of fabric.

3 Thread your needle with white sewing thread. Starting with a few small stitches to secure the thread, sew running stitch (see page 9) close to the edge all the way around a circle of fabric, using quite big stitches.

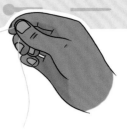

4 When you have stitched all the way around the circle, gently pull the thread— the fabric will gather up into a flower.

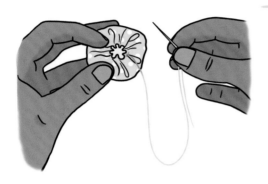

5 Keep pulling until the fabric is pulled together into a very small circle. Finish with a few small stitches and then flatten the flower with your hand. Repeat steps 3–5 with the remaining circles of fabric.

6 Photocopy the leaf template on page 123 or trace it onto scrap paper, and cut it out. Fold the green felt in half and pin the paper leaf to it. Cut around the paper leaf shape and take the pin out. Pin the paper shape to the felt again and cut out another leaf shape. You will have four felt leaves.

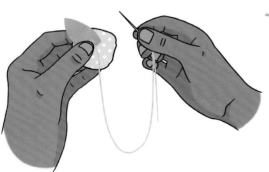

7 Turn a flower over, sew a few small stitches in the middle on the back to secure the thread, then stitch through the base of a felt leaf. Sew back and forth through the center of the flower and the leaf a few times so that they are firmly joined together. Don't cut the thread or take the needle out, as you'll need them to stitch on the button.

Tip

Don't worry about your stitches showing on the front of the flower, because they'll be covered by the button in the next step.

Put on your dancing SHOES!

8 Bring the needle and thread through to the front of the flower and thread it through one of the holes on a button. Push it back through the other hole (or across the diagonal if there are four holes). Continue to stitch the button in place (see page 11) and finish with a few small stitches on the back of the flower. Do the same with the other flowers.

9 Using fabric glue, attach the flower decorations to your shoes, gluing two flowers to each shoe. Let the glue dry completely (this may take a few hours) before wearing your shoes.

Fruit Brooches

Jazz up your jacket with these fun, fruity brooches.
They're made from colorful felt, which is very easy to use
and doesn't fray. Brooch pins are available from good craft stores,
but you could use a large safety pin securely stitched to the back if
you can't get hold of any.

You will need

Templates on page 123

For the watermelon

4-in. (10-cm) square of dark green felt

3½ x 2 in. (9 x 5 cm) white felt

3 x 2 in. (8 x 5 cm) red felt

Green sewing thread

Black embroidery floss (thread)

Polyester toy stuffing

Brooch pin

For the orange

4-in. (10-cm) square of orange felt

3½ x 2 in. (9 x 5 cm) white felt

3 x 2 in. (8 x 5 cm) paler orange felt

Orange sewing thread

Polyester toy stuffing

Brooch pin

For the lime

4-in. (10-cm) square of lime-green felt

3½ x 2 in. (9 x 5 cm) white felt

3 x 2 in. (8 x 5 cm) paler lime-green felt

Lime-green sewing thread

Polyester toy stuffing

Brooch pin

Scissors

Paper

Pencil

Pins

Sewing and embroidery needles

To Make the Watermelon

1 Enlarge the templates on page 123 by 200% and cut out pieces A, B, and C.

2 Fold the 4-in. (10-cm) square of green felt in half and pin pattern piece A to it. Cut it out carefully, then take the pin and paper off so that you have two green pieces.

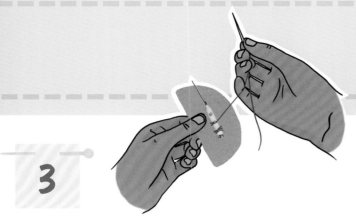

3

Thread a needle with sewing thread to match the green felt. Take one of the pieces and sew a few small stitches to the middle of it to secure the thread. Then sew the brooch pin to it, sewing through the holes in the back of the pin and over the metal bar. You may find it easier to open the pin to sew it in place, but be careful not to prick your fingers. Finish with a few small stitches.

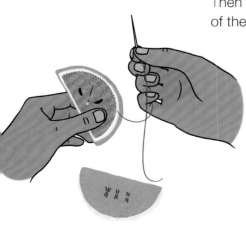

4 Pin pattern piece B to the white felt and carefully cut it out. Pin pattern piece C to the red felt and carefully cut it out. Take off the pins and paper.

FRUITY favorites

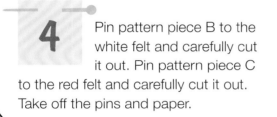

5 Thread your needle with black embroidery floss (thread) and tie a knot in the end. Take the red piece, push your needle up from the back of the felt to the front, and sew three small straight stitches to look like melon seeds. Then push the needle through to the back of the felt and finish with another knot.

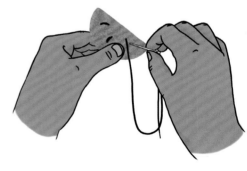

6 Take the front green A piece (the one without the brooch pin) and pin the red and white parts to it, matching up the straight edges and checking there is an even border of green and white at each end. Thread your needle with red sewing thread. Starting and finishing with a few small stitches, make small straight stitches around the curved edge of the red felt, stitching through all three layers.

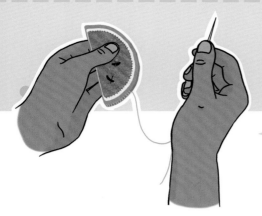

7 Put the green piece with the brooch pin on the table, pin side down, and place the other layers, right side up, on top of it. Pin all the layers together. Starting and finishing with a few small stitches, whipstitch (see page 10) almost all the way around the felt, leaving a gap of 1–2 in. (2.5–5 cm) open. Take the pins out, but don't cut the thread or pull the needle out, as you'll need them again in the next step.

8 Fill the shape with a little stuffing (you won't need very much) and then continue sewing and finish with a few small stitches to hold the thread in place.

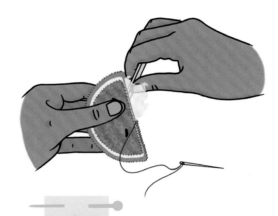

To Make the Orange and Lime

The orange and lime are made in a similar way, but using a dark shade of orange or lime green for the A pieces, white for the B pieces, and a paler shade of lime or orange for the D segment pieces.

9 Start in the same way as for the watermelon—you will need the D template this time. Fold the darker orange or lime-green felt in half and cut two A pieces. Then cut one white B piece and three paler orange or lime-green D pieces. Sew the brooch pin to one of the dark A pieces, as in step 3.

10 Take the front A piece (the one without the brooch pin) and pin the white felt and the small D parts to it, matching up the straight edges and checking there is an even border at each end. Thread your needle with sewing thread to match the D pieces. Starting and finishing with a few small stitches, make small straight stitches around the D pieces, stitching through all three layers. For the middle D piece, stitch around all three edges; for the other two pieces you don't need to stitch along the top straight edges.

11 Put the back felt A piece (the one with the brooch pin) on the table, pin side down, and place the other layers right side up on top. Follow the instructions in steps 7 and 8 to sew them together and stuff them.

Mittens

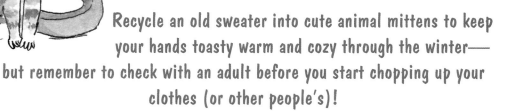

Recycle an old sweater into cute animal mittens to keep your hands toasty warm and cozy through the winter— but remember to check with an adult before you start chopping up your clothes (or other people's)!

You will need

Templates on page 123

An old woolen sweater

Black, pink, and white yarn (wool) or embroidery floss (thread)

Paper

Pencil

Scissors

Pins

Yarn (darning) needle

1 Enlarge the templates on page 123 by 200%. Cut out a paper mitten shape and a paper ear shape.

2 Pin the paper mitten shape to the bottom of the sweater so that the straight edge of the paper lines up with the bottom of the sweater, pinning through both the front and the back of the sweater. Pin it near the side edge, so that you leave plenty of room to cut out the second mitten. Cut around the template, but keep the pieces pinned together; now you've got a front and a back piece for the first mitten. Then turn the template over, so that the thumb is pointing in the opposite direction. Pin it onto the sweater and cut out two more mitten shapes for the second mitten.

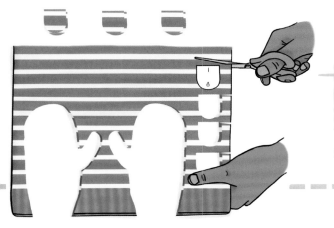

3 Pin the paper ear shape to the sweater, again pinning through both the front and the back, and cut around it. Do this three more times so that you have eight woolen ear shapes.

4 Pin two ear shapes right sides together. Thread your needle with white yarn (wool) or embroidery floss (thread) and tie a knot in the end. Backstitch (see page 10) all around the curved edge, leaving the straight bottom edge open, and finish with another knot.

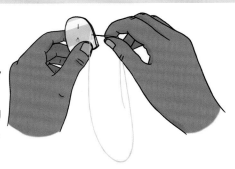

5 Turn the ear right side out. Repeat steps 4 and 5 with the other ears, so that you have four in total.

6 Place the two sets of mitten pieces on the table in front of you, with the thumbs pointing inward. The top layer of each set is the front of the mitten. Take the pins out of one set and put the back piece to one side for now. Thread the needle with black yarn or embroidery floss and tie a knot in the end. Working from the back to the front, make two stitches in a cross shape on the front mitten piece to make an eye and then stitch another eye about ⅝ in. (1.5 cm) from the first one. Finish with a knot on the back.

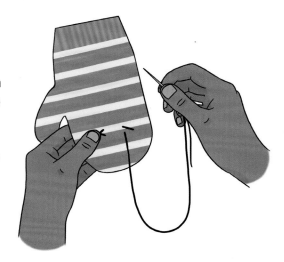

7 Using pink yarn or embroidery floss, sew a nose on by making three straight stitches, each one a bit shorter than the last. Then use white yarn or floss to sew two straight lines in a V-shape for whiskers on either side of the nose. Start and finish each color with a knot on the back.

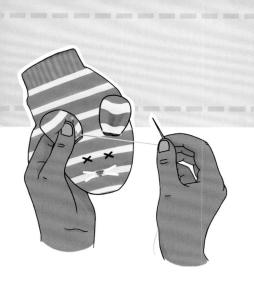

8 Take an ear and tuck the raw edge inside. Tie a knot in the end of some white yarn or floss and stitch a few running stitches (see page 10) across the bottom of the ear, then pull the yarn to gather the ear a bit. Stitch it onto the embroidered mitten front. Repeat with another ear so that they are both stitched in place.

9 Lay the embroidered mitten right side up on your table, then place the back mitten piece from this pair right side down on top. Pin them together all the way round, leaving the cuff open. Using white yarn or floss, and starting and finishing with a knot, backstitch them together. Turn the mitten right side out.

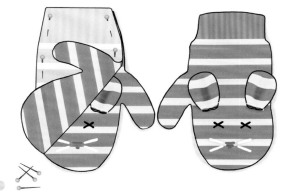

10 Now lay the mitten you have finished down on the table so that the face is looking at you and put the other set of pieces beside it so that the thumbs are pointing inward, toward each other. Pick up the top piece of the second mitten and repeat steps 6–7 to make a second face. (You don't want to stitch the face to the wrong side!) Add the ears, and sew the back and the front of the mitten together as before. Now try on your mittens for size!

Padded Necklace ☺ ○ ○

Don't throw your scraps of fabric away—use them to make this lovely necklace so that nothing will go to waste. Cut circles of patterned fabrics, stitch them together, and pad with stuffing to make the beads, then thread them onto cord, making sure that the necklace will fit over your head before you tie the knot.

You will need

Eight pieces of fabric, each at least 2½ x 5 in. (6 x 12 cm)

White sewing thread

Polyester toy stuffing

26 in. (65 cm) thin cord

Four beads, about ⅜ in. (1 cm) in diameter

Ruler

Small pot to draw around

Paper

Pencil

Scissors

Pins

Sewing needle

Yarn (darning) needle (for threading the cord)

1 Use the template on page 123 or find a small pot that measures about 1½ in. (4 cm) across; spice pots are about this size. Draw around it carefully on paper and then put it back where you found it! Cut out the circle.

2 Fold one piece of fabric in half. Pin the paper circle to it and cut it out carefully. Take off the pin and paper and you will have two circles of fabric. Do the same with the seven other fabrics.

3 Thread the needle with white sewing thread. Put two of the circles together, with the right side of the fabric facing outward; you can either use two of the same fabric circles together or mix them up so that each side of the beads will be different. Starting with a few small stitches to hold the thread in place, sew running stitch (see page 9) about three-quarters of the way around the circle. Don't cut the thread or pull the needle out—you haven't finished with them yet!

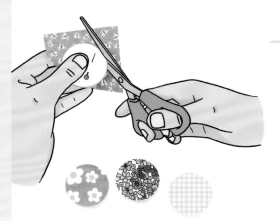

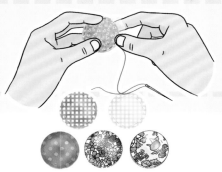

4 Push a small piece of stuffing between the two circles of fabric, then stitch the rest of the way around, finishing with a few more small stitches. Sew all the pairs of circles in the same way so that you have eight padded beads.

5 Thread the yarn (darning) needle with cord and push it through the middle of each padded bead from one side to the other, between the layers of fabric. Leave about ⅜ in. (1 cm) between each bead, and leave an equal amount of cord at each end of the necklace.

A scrap stash NECKLACE

6 When all the beads are threaded onto the cord, take out the needle. Put the necklace around your neck to work out how long you want the cord to be, so you can take the necklace off and put it on over your head. Then tie the ends together in a knot, leaving at least 2 in. (5 cm) or so of cord free.

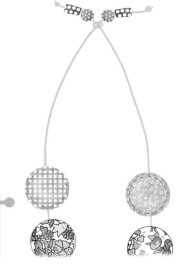

7 Thread two beads onto each end of the cord, then tie a large knot to hold the beads in place. Trim the ends of the cord if you need to.

Champp's T-shirt

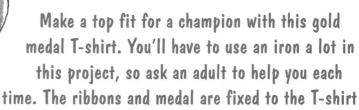

Make a top fit for a champion with this gold medal T-shirt. You'll have to use an iron a lot in this project, so ask an adult to help you each time. The ribbons and medal are fixed to the T-shirt with fusible bonding web, but stitching around them as well will help to keep your T-shirt looking good for longer.

You will need

11 x 8 in. (28 x 20 cm) fusible bonding web

11 x 4 in. (28 x 10cm) stripy fabric

4-in. (10-cm) square of yellow fabric

3½-in. (9-cm) square of spotty fabric

3 x 2 in. (8 x 5 cm) blue spotty fabric

Plain white T-shirt

Template on page 123

Iron

Ruler

Pencil

Scissors

Ironing board

Iron

Pair of compasses

Paper

Pinking shears

Pins

Needle and white sewing thread

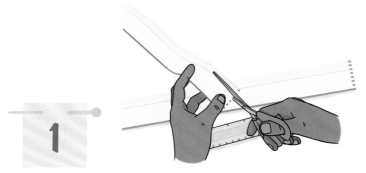

1 Ask an adult to help you and, following the manufacturer's instructions, use an iron to attach fusible bonding web to the back of the stripy fabric. Using a ruler and pencil, draw two rectangles measuring 10½ x 1 in. (27 x 2.5 cm) on the bonding-web side of the fabric. Cut them out.

2 Place the T-shirt on an ironing board. Peel off the backing paper from the bonding-web rectangles. Lay the two rectangles on the T-shirt to look like ribbons, with the bonding-web side facing down, overlapping the ends a little bit. Place a damp cloth over the top and ask an adult to help you press the rectangles with a medium-hot iron. Check that the fabrics have bonded to the T-shirt; if they have not, replace the damp cloth and press for a little longer.

The WINNER!

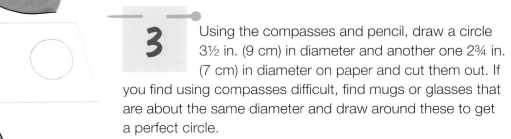

3 Using the compasses and pencil, draw a circle 3½ in. (9 cm) in diameter and another one 2¾ in. (7 cm) in diameter on paper and cut them out. If you find using compasses difficult, find mugs or glasses that are about the same diameter and draw around these to get a perfect circle.

4 Cut two pieces of bonding web to fit the squares of yellow and spotty fabric and ask an adult to help you press them onto the back of the fabrics, as before. Pin the larger paper circle to the yellow fabric, draw around it, and cut it out with pinking shears. Pin the smaller circle to the spotty fabric, draw around it, and cut it out with ordinary scissors.

5 Peel the backing paper off both circles of fabric. Place the larger circle over the ends of the stripy fabric "ribbons." Place a damp cloth over the top and press it, as before. Let the fabric cool down, then put the smaller circle in the middle of the larger one and press it in place in the same way.

6 Photocopy the template on page 123 or trace it onto scrap paper, and cut out a number "one." Cut a piece of bonding web to fit the piece of blue spotty fabric and press it onto the back of the fabric, as before. Turn the paper number over so that it is the wrong way round (this is very important, or your number one will be back to front when you cut it out!), pin it to the back of the blue spotty fabric, and draw around it. Take off the paper number and cut out the fabric number.

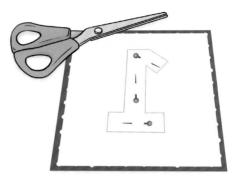

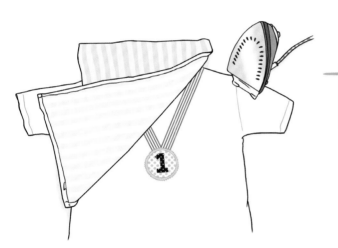

7

Peel off the backing paper from the number, then place it on the medal and press it in place, as before.

8 Thread your needle with white sewing thread. Sew running stitch (see page 9) around the edges of the circles and ribbons, starting with a few small stitches on the back. Make sure that you do not sew through the back of the T-shirt as well! Putting a piece of card inside the T-shirt will stop you from doing this.

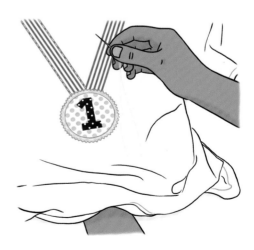

Hat Rosettes

Brighten up a plain hat with these fun fabric rosettes. Glue them onto a straw summer hat or stitch them onto a knitted winter hat to add a personalized detail. You can use the rosettes to decorate all sorts of things—a plain bag, a pencil case, greetings cards, hair ties... the possibilities are endless!

You will need

14 x 2 in. (36 x 5 cm) spotty fabric

14 x 1½ in. (36 x 4 cm) each of two other spotty fabrics

3 co-ordinating buttons— one ⅞ in. (22 mm) and two ¾ in. (2 cm) in diameter

White sewing thread

Hat

Pinking shears

Sewing needle

Fabric glue

1 Using pinking shears, cut along one long side of each piece of fabric, cutting about ¼ in. (5 mm) from the edge. This will give the rosettes a nice frilly edge and will stop the fabric from fraying.

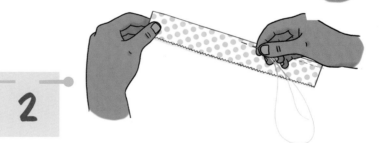

2 Thread your needle with white sewing thread. Sew a few small stitches at the end of one of the pieces of fabric, close to the long straight edge, to secure the thread in place. Sew running stitch (see page 9) all the way along the straight edge. When you get to the end, leave the needle in place—and don't secure the thread.

3 Gently pull the thread: the fabric will gather up. You'll need to tweak the gathers with your fingers to make them even. When the fabric is completely gathered along the bottom edge and curls around to make a circle, sew a few stitches to join the bottom corners into a ring. Finish with a few small stitches this time—but don't cut the thread or take the needle out just yet.

4 Fluff the rosette out with your fingers a little to make a nice shape.

5 Using the needle and thread that you left in step 3, sew a button to the middle of the rosette (see page 11). Repeat steps 1–5 to make two more rosettes in the same way, using the other pieces of fabric.

6 Using fabric glue, stitch the rosettes to the hat. Make sure you leave the glue to dry completely before you wear the hat. This may take a couple of hours. If you prefer, you could stitch the rosettes onto a wooly hat.

chapter 2
Toys and Dolls

Felt Mice

Make an adorable felt mouse to play with and then tuck it up in its own bed for a good night's sleep. Use scraps of patterned fabric for the ears and add bows, embroidered eyeglasses, and buttons to give your mouse a special personality. Once you've made it, decorate a large matchbox with pretty fabric and braid to make a comfy bed. You could go on to create a whole family of mice!

For one mouse you will need

Templates on page 124

8 x 6 in. (20 x 15 cm) white or gray felt for the mouse's body

Scraps of patterned fabric for the inner ears and bed

2 tiny beads for eyes

2 small buttons

Handful of polyester toy stuffing

Piece of narrow ribbon about 6 in. (15 cm) long for a bow

Selection of ribbons and braids to decorate the bed

Pink and black embroidery floss (thread)

White or gray sewing thread

Large empty matchbox for the bed

Pencil

Ruler

Scissors

Pins

Sewing and embroidery needles

Fabric glue

1 Enlarge the templates on page 124 by 200% and cut them out. Pin the front, back, and head templates onto felt and cut them out carefully. Take out the pins and remove the templates.

2 Place the head on the front felt piece, lining them up neatly at the top. Pin them together at the top. Starting and finishing with a few small stitches on the wrong side (the back of the front piece), sew two beads onto the head for eyes, sewing through both layers of felt.

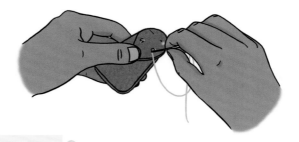

3 If you are adding eyeglasses, thread a needle with black embroidery floss (thread) and tie a knot in the end. Push the needle through from the back of the mouse to the front and backstitch a circle around each eye (see page 10). Then add a single stitch between the circles and a few more stitches on either side. Finish with another knot or a few small stitches on the wrong side.

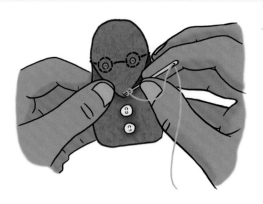

4 Thread a needle with pink embroidery floss and tie a knot in the end. Push the needle through from the back of the mouse to the front, so that it comes out near the tip of the nose. Make a French knot (see page 10) and finish with another knot or a few small stitches on the wrong side. Stitch buttons onto the front of the mouse if you are using them.

5 Fold the patterned fabric over so that it is double, and pin the template for the inner ear to it. Cut the inner ears out neatly, then take out the pin and remove the template. Place the inner ears on top of the felt ears and pin them in place.

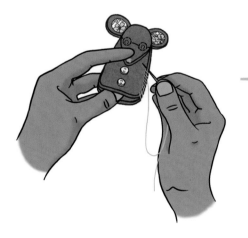

6 Put the front of the mouse on the back, lining up the edges carefully, and pin the layers together. Whipstitch around the sides and head of the mouse (see page 10), making sure that the needle goes through all the layers. Leave the bottom edge open so that you can stuff the mouse! Across the bottom of the ears (where you won't be able to make whipstitches), make a few small running stitches, making sure you catch in the inner-ear fabric as you sew.

7 Take a few small pieces of stuffing and fill the mouse, making sure there are no lumps or bumps. Make sure it's nice and plump!

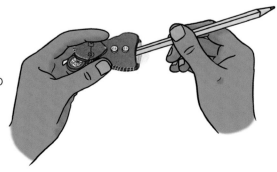

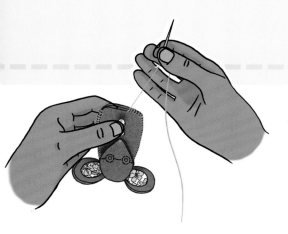

8 Whipstitch the opening closed, remembering to start and finish with a few small stitches.

9 If you're adding a ribbon bow to your mouse, fold the ribbon in half to find the center and stitch the center of the ribbon onto the center of the top of the head with a few small stitches over and over. Then tie the ribbon in a neat bow.

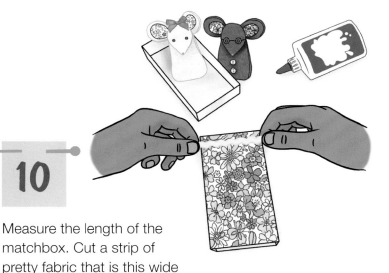

10 Measure the length of the matchbox. Cut a strip of pretty fabric that is this wide and long enough to cover the sides and top of the box. Glue it onto the box. Fold another piece of fabric and slip it inside to make a nice, soft mattress for your mouse. When the glue has dried, glue strips of ribbon or braid to the outside of the box to make it extra special.

Is your MOUSE asleep?

Maurice the Moose

Whenever you are in your room Maurice will be there, looking down from the wall to make you smile. He doesn't need much stitching—just some buttons and some running stitch to hold on his antlers.

You will need

Large stripy adult sock for the head

Small pair of child's gloves for the antlers

Polyester toy stuffing

Embroidery floss (thread) to match the antlers

Two white buttons for the eyes

Large red button for the nose

White and red sewing thread

Small piece of ribbon or cord to hang

5-in. (13-cm) embroidery hoop

Pins

Embroidery and sewing needles

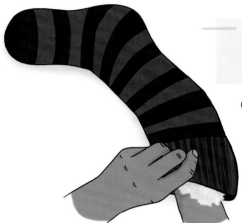

1 Fill the sock with stuffing, pushing it down into the toe and making sure it doesn't look lumpy.

2 Stuff the gloves to make antlers, pushing the stuffing into the fingers so that the gloves stand upright. Both antlers should look the same, so have a good look at them when you've finished—you may need to add more stuffing or take some stuffing out.

3 Thread a needle with embroidery floss (thread) and tie a knot in the end. Keeping the wrist part of the glove open in a circle, pin an antler onto the top of the head and stitch it in place using running stitches (see page 9). You can make the stitches quite big! Finish with a knot in the thread. Sew the second antler on in the same way.

4

Thread a sewing needle with white thread, then sew buttons onto the moose's head to look like eyes (see page 11). Now use red thread to sew on a big red button for the nose. Make sure all the buttons are stitched on firmly.

5

Undo the screw on the embroidery hoop and separate the inner and outer rings. Thread the ribbon or cord that you are using through the outer hoop. Tie it in a knot to make a loop to hang the moose on the wall.

6

Stretch the cuff of the sock over the inner ring of the embroidery hoop, pulling it so that it sits firmly over the hoop and the moose's head is upright. If it is a long sock, you will have to push the ring right inside it so that the moose's neck is not too long.

7

Place the outer ring over the inner ring and the sock cuff, then tighten the screw. You can push any extra-long sock back inside or cut it off. Ask an adult to help you hang the moose on the wall using the cord or ribbon loop.

Felt Bugs

Make yourself a crazy bug collection with these funny felt creatures. They are very easy to make, because you only need to use running stitch and sew on buttons. Choose brightly colored pieces of felt and cut out spots and stripes or add your own decorations and designs. Why not make some for your friends, too? They'll be amazed that you made them all by yourself!

You will need

Templates on page 124

8-in. (20-cm) square of felt for the body

5-in. (13-cm) square of felt for wings or legs

4-in. (10-cm) square of felt for spots or stripes

2 buttons for eyes

Sewing threads to match the felt colors

Polyester toy stuffing

Pencil

Scissors

Pins

Sewing needle

1 Enlarge the templates on page 124 by 200% and cut them out. Fold the largest piece of felt in half and pin the body template to it. Cut it out neatly; this will give you a front body piece and a back body piece.

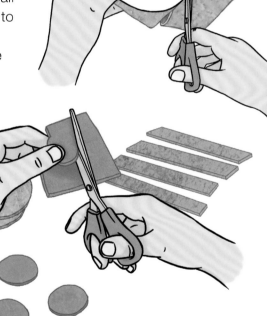

Tip

Cut the stripes a bit longer than you need. Once you've stitched them in place, you can trim them so that they're level with the edge of the bug's body.

2 Cut out stripes or spots from the smallest square of felt, making sure that they will fit onto the body. Arrange them on one of the body pieces and pin them in place.

Big, bright, beautiful BUGS!

3 Thread a needle with sewing thread to match the spots or stripes, then knot the end. Push the needle through from the back of the felt to the front, then stitch the spots or stripes in place with running stitch (see page 9). Finish with a few small stitches on the wrong side. Take the pins out. Stitch two buttons onto the body to look like eyes (see page 11).

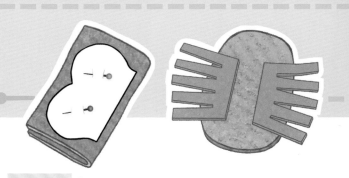

4 Fold the 5-in. (13-cm) square of felt in half. Using the templates, cut out two wings or two lots of legs. Put them on the remaining body piece—you don't need to pin them, as they'll be held in place by the stitching in the next step.

5 Put the top body piece on the bottom piece, lining up the edges. Pin them together. Thread a needle with sewing thread to match the body, then knot the end. Push the needle in between the two layers of felt and bring it out on the top of the bug, about ⅛ in. (3 mm) from the edge, so that the knot is hidden in the middle. Work running stitches all the way around, leaving a gap of about 1½ in. (4 cm) in the back end of the bug. Don't cut the thread or pull the needle out, as you'll need them again to finish the sewing!

6 Push stuffing in through the gap, pushing it right down to the end and spreading it around so that the bug is evenly stuffed. You can use the blunt end of a pencil to push the stuffing in.

7 Sew up the gap with more running stitches, finishing with a few small stitches on the underside of the bug.

Teddy Bear

Everyone needs a bear to hug, and this cute creature is so simple that you can make it yourself. Choose soft, fluffy fleece fabric in pale gray like this one—or go for a bright fleece in your favorite color, finishing off with a co-ordinating ribbon.

You will need

Template on page 125

20 x 15 in. (50 x 40 cm) fleece fabric

Black embroidery floss (thread)

Sewing thread to match the fleece fabric

Polyester toy stuffing

15 in. (40 cm) ribbon, 1 in. (2.5 cm) wide

Scissors

Paper

Pencil

Pins

Sewing and embroidery needles

Air-soluble marker pen (optional)

1 Enlarge the template on page 125 by 200% and cut it out. Fold the fleece fabric in half and pin the paper pattern to it. Carefully cut around the paper pattern and then take the pins out. You will have two fleece bear shapes—one for the front and one for the back.

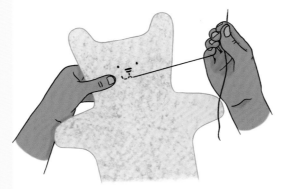

2 Thread a needle with black embroidery floss (thread) and tie a knot in the end. Take one of the fleece bear shapes and push the needle through from the back of the fabric to the front. Stitch two French knots for eyes, two small stitches for a nose, and a few small backstitches for a mouth (see page 10). Finish with a knot on the wrong side again.

Tip

The template on page 125 shows where the bear's eyes, nose, and mouth go. If you wish, you can trace them onto the bear's head with an air-soluble marker pen so that you can just stitch over the lines. The marker pen lines will fade away, so draw them on just before you start stitching!

3 Put the embroidered bear shape right side up on the table, then put the other fleece bear shape right side down on top (so that the bear's face is on the inside). Pin the two layers together.

4 Thread your needle with sewing thread to match the fleece fabric. Starting and finishing with a few small stitches, backstitch almost all the way around the bear shape, leaving a gap of about 2 in. (5 cm) along one side.

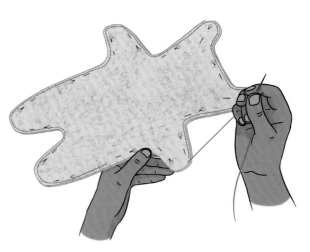

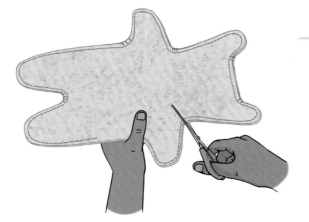

5 Where there's a deep curve in the bear shape—under and above the arms, at the start of the ears, and between the legs—use sharp scissors to make small snips from the outside edge toward the stitches. Take care not to snip through the stitches! This will help to give the bear a nice shape.

6 Turn the bear right side out, carefully pulling it through the opening. Use the blunt end of a pencil to push out the arms, legs, ears, and head.

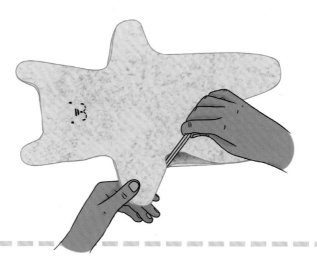

Take care of your BEAR

7 Take small pieces of stuffing and fill the bear, pushing the stuffing into the arms, legs, and head to make a nice round bear. When the bear is stuffed, stitch the opening closed with whipstitches (see page 10), starting and finishing with a few small stitches to hold the thread in place. Tie a ribbon in a neat bow around your bear's neck to finish.

Teddy Bear Snuggle Sack

Once you have made your little bear, he'll need a comfy bed to sleep in—so why not make this snuggle sack, which doubles as a sleepover bag? With room to keep your nightwear, toothbrush, and other sleepover essentials in, you and your bear will both get a good night's sleep!

You will need

Two 11 x 12½ in. (28 x 32 cm) pieces of fabric for the outer bag

11 x 17 in. (28 x 44 cm) fabric for the pocket

Two 11 x 12½ in. (28 x 32 cm) pieces of fabric for the lining

Two 12 x 4 in. (30 x 10 cm) pieces of fabric for the handles

6 x 7 in. (15 x 18 cm) fabric for the pillow (optional)

Polyester toy stuffing for the pillow (optional)

Sewing thread to match the fabric

Scissors

Pencil

Pins

Sewing needle

Safety pin

1 Take one piece of the outer bag fabric and lay it right side up on the table. Take the pocket fabric and lay it right side down on top of this, lining up the bottom and sides of the two fabrics. Fold the top of the pocket fabric down to meet the bottom. The pocket fabric is now folded in half, with the right side out and the fold at the top.

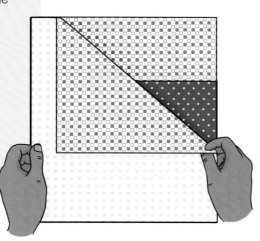

2 Put the other outer bag piece right side down on top of this, matching up the edges of the fabric pieces.

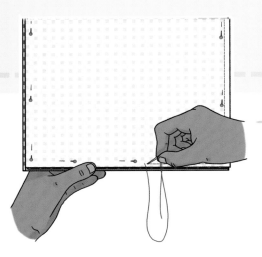

3 Pin around the sides and across the bottom, leaving the top open. Thread your needle with sewing thread to match the fabric. Backstitch (see page 10) along these three sides, starting and finishing with a few small stitches to hold the thread in place. Take the pins out.

4 Place the two pieces of fabric for the lining together, with the right sides facing inward. Pin around the sides and across the bottom, leaving the top open. Starting and finishing with a few small stitches, backstitch along the side and bottom edges—but this time leave a gap of about 2 in. (5 cm) along the bottom edge. Take the pins out.

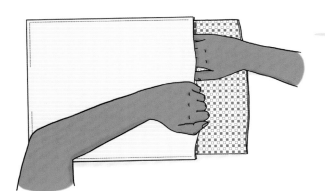

5 Turn the outer bag right side out (so that the pocket is on the outside). Slip the lining bag over it (the right sides will be together). Line up the top edge and the side seams, pushing the corners of the outer bag into the corners of the lining. Pin the lining and outer bags together all the way around the top.

6 Starting and finishing with a few small stitches, backstitch all around the top of the bag. Take the pins out.

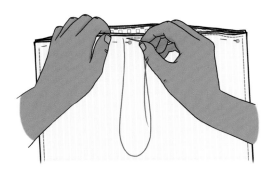

7 Turn the whole bag right side out by pulling the bag through the gap in the stitching at the bottom of the lining. You will have a long tube.

8 Where you left the gap in the lining in step 4, fold both edges of the fabric in until they're level with the stitched edge around the bottom edge of the bag. Starting and finishing with a few small stitches, whipstitch the gap closed (see page 10).

9 Push the lining inside the bag and push the corners out carefully with your fingers so that they look nice and neat. Ask an adult to help you press the bag with an iron.

10 Take the two pieces of fabric for the handles and fold them both in half lengthwise. Ask an adult to help you press them with an iron. Pin along the long open edge of each handle and then backstitch all the way along to make two tubes. Take the pins out.

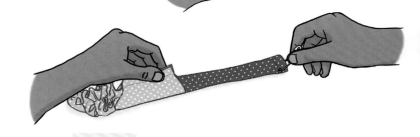

11 Pin a safety pin through one end of one of the fabric tubes and then push the pin back through the tube until it comes out of the other end. As you push it through, you can gradually turn the fabric the right way out. This can be a bit fiddly. Do the same with the second tube.

Why not make a pillow to make your bear even cozier? Fold the fabric in half, pin along one short end and the long unfolded side, and backstitch along them. Keep the needle threaded and turn the pillow to the right way out. Fill the pillowcase with stuffing, then turn the fabric at the open short end in by ⅜ in. (1 cm) and whipstitch it closed, finishing with a few small stitches to hold the thread in place.

A bag for a BEAR and other bits

12 On the front of the bag, measure 2 in. (5 cm) from one side seam and mark with a pencil. Measure and make another mark 2 in. (5 cm) from the other side. Turn the bag over and do the same on the back. Turn the ends of the handles under by ⅝ in. (1.5 cm) and pin them to the top of the outside of the bag, so that the edge nearest the seam just covers the marks you have made. Thread your needle and pull the thread right through so that it is double before knotting it at the end, to make it strong for the handle. Starting and finishing with a few small stitches on the inside of the bag, sew small running stitches (see page 9) in a rectangle where the handle is doubled over.

Felt Vegetables

Play shop with your very own handmade felt vegetables! This is a lovely project if you're new to sewing, as the shapes are all easy to make. If you enjoy making these, then why not stitch other fruits and vegetables? Try apples, strawberries, and peppers, drawing the shapes yourself and making them in the same way.

You will need

Templates on pages 124–25

For the carrot

6-in. (15-cm) square of orange felt and matching embroidery floss (thread)

3-in. (8-cm) square of green felt

For the eggplant (aubergine)

7-in. (18-cm) square of purple felt and matching embroidery floss

3-in. (8-cm) square of green felt and matching embroidery floss

For the radish

5 x 3 in. (13 x 8 cm) pink felt and matching embroidery floss

3 x 2½ in. (8 x 6 cm) green felt

For the tomato

7 x 4 in. (18 x 10 cm) red felt and matching embroidery floss

4 x 3 in. (10 x 8 cm) green felt and matching embroidery floss

For the lettuce

Three 7-in. (18-cm) squares of felt in different shades of green and green embroidery floss

Needle

Scissors

Paper

Pins

Polyester toy stuffing

Cutting out the pieces

1 Enlarge the templates on pages 124–25 by 200% and cut them out.

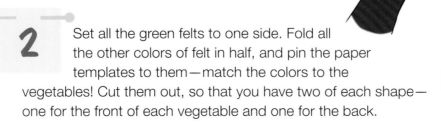

2 Set all the green felts to one side. Fold all the other colors of felt in half, and pin the paper templates to them—match the colors to the vegetables! Cut them out, so that you have two of each shape— one for the front of each vegetable and one for the back.

3 Now pin the green stalk and leaf patterns to the green felts and cut them out carefully so that you have one of each. No need to fold the felt in half this time!

To make the eggplant (aubergine) and tomato

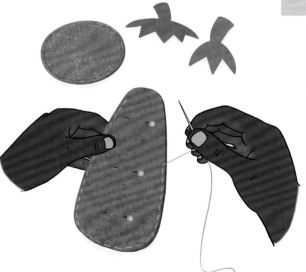

1 Pin the front and back piece of each vegetable together. Thread your needle with embroidery floss (thread) to match the felt, and tie a knot in the end. Stitch around each shape with running stitch (see page 9), leaving a gap in the stitching of about 2 in. (5 cm) at the top. Take the pins out—but don't cut the thread or take the needle out, as you'll need them again later.

2

Take small pieces of stuffing and push them into the felt shapes, being careful not to prick your finger on the threaded needle. When you have filled the shapes, carry on stitching running stitch around the shape to close the gap, finishing with a knot.

3 Take the green felt stalk for each vegetable and pin it in place at the top. Starting and finishing with a knot in the thread, stitch the stalk in place with running stitch.

To make the radish and carrot

1 Take the green felt leaves for each vegetable and put them on the back pieces. Place the front pieces on top and pin all the layers together.

2

Thread your needle with embroidery floss to match the felt. Starting and finishing with a knot, stitch running stitch all around the vegetables, making sure you sew through all the layers. As with the eggplant and tomato, leave a gap of about 2 in. (5 cm) for stuffing along one side edge. Take the pins out—but don't cut the thread or take the needle out, as you'll need them again later.

3 Fill the shapes with stuffing and then continue to stitch, ending with a knot.

To make the lettuce

1 Using the pattern piece, cut out one shape from each of the three green felt pieces, so that you have three felt shapes—each in a different shade.

2 Fold each shape in half and then in quarters and lay them on top of each other.

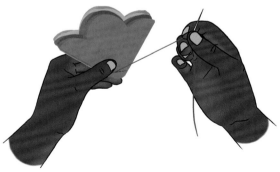

3 Tie a knot in the end of the thread. Stitch across the bottom corner through all the layers, making a few stitches to hold them all firmly together, and finish with a knot. Open out the leaves slightly to form the lettuce.

Dog Finger Puppets

Dog lovers will go crazy for these fun finger puppets! Choose a pedigree pup or make up your own mongrel. You can add big droopy ears or little pointy ones, and sew on patches around the eyes, to create your own range of canine characters.

For one puppet you will need

Templates on page 125

7-in. (18-cm) square of brown, gray, or white felt for the head and body

Scraps of felt for nose, ears, and patches

Black thread

Embroidery floss (thread) in your chosen color for the eyes

Paper

Pencil

Scissors

Pins

Sewing and embroidery needles

1 Enlarge the templates on page 125 by 200% and cut out paper shapes for the body, head, nose, ears, and any of the other features that you would like to use.

2 Pin the head template onto the square of felt, placing it near the edge. Then fold the rest of the felt in half so that it's doubled, and pin the body template to it. Cut around the templates so that you have one head and two bodies.

3 Pin the nose template onto black felt and cut it out. Thread a sewing needle with black thread. Starting and finishing with a few small stitches and making a few stitches across the nose, stitch the nose onto the head. If you are making the dark brown dog, cut out the cheeks section from contrasting felt and pin it in place before you sew on the nose. When you've finished, take out the pins.

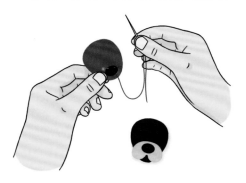

Tip

For tiny pieces like the nose, ears, and patches, it is sometimes easier to draw around the templates and then cut out along the lines.

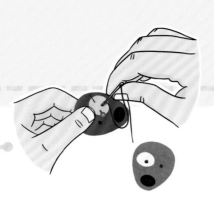

4

Thread an embroidery needle with floss (thread) and tie a knot in the end. Working from the back of the head to the front, stitch two French knots (see page 10) for eyes. Finish with a knot on the back. If you want to add a patch around one eye, cut one out of a contrasting color of felt and pin it onto the face, then sew a French knot through it.

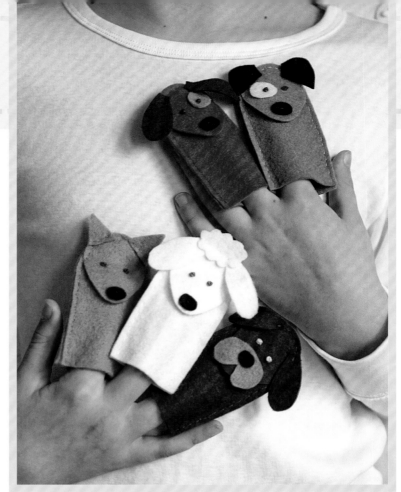

yap-yap... woof-woof... HOWL!

5

Put the two body pieces together, with the head on top. Pin the layers together all the way around. Using thread to match the felt, and starting and finishing with a few small stitches on the back, backstitch (see page 10) neatly all the way around, leaving the bottom edge open.

6

Cut out ears in the color and shape that you would like. Thread a sewing needle with thread to match the felt. Starting and finishing with a few small stitches on the back to secure the thread, stitch the ears onto the head, adding the extra pom-pom shape if you're making the white dog.

Clothes-pin Dolls

These sweet dolls are fun to make and great fun to play with. Make a knight, superhero, queen, or ballerina like these or come up with your own characters, using scraps of fabric and beads and buttons. You can buy these old-fashioned wooden clothes pins from some hardware stores, but you are more likely to find them at craft stores. Look for pins with wooden bases made specially for craft projects, which will stand up, too.

You will need

Wooden clothes pins

Acrylic paint in different colors

Pieces of fabric at least
6 x 3 in. (15 x 8 cm)

Scraps of ribbon, sequins, and rick-rack

Embroidery floss (thread)

Small paintbrushes

Felt-tip pens for the face

Pinking shears

Needle

Fast-drying water-based glue

Scissors

1 Decide which doll you would like to make and paint the clothes pin in the colors you want to use. Look at these dolls as a guide or make up your own characters and designs.

2 When the paint has dried, draw the face on with felt-tip pens.

3 To make the clothes, cut a piece of fabric using pinking shears. (If you're using felt, ordinary scissors will be fine.) You'll need a piece measuring about 6 x 3 in. (15 x 8 cm) for a cloak and 6 x 2 in. (15 x 5 cm) for a skirt.

4 Thread the needle with embroidery floss (thread), but don't tie a knot in the end. Push the needle into the fabric and pull it through until there's about 2 in. (5 cm) sticking out at the end. Sew running stitch (see page 9) along one long edge of the fabric.

5 Take off the needle and gently pull both ends of the floss to gather the fabric up. Put the cloak or skirt around the clothes pin, tie the ends of the floss in a knot, and trim the ends.

6 Add any other decorations (sequins, beads, glitter etc.) you like, sticking them in place with glue. Let the glue dry completely before you play with your dolls.

Mermaid

Make a rag doll with a difference—a pretty mermaid complete with golden hair and crown. This project involves quite a lot of sewing so it may take you a while to finish, but it isn't complicated—and when you're through, you'll have a lovely new toy to treasure. Try different colors of fabric and look for plain cottons in skin tones to give your mermaid a different look.

You will need

Templates on page 126

11-in. (28-cm) square of spotty fabric

11-in. (28-cm) square of calico (muslin) or plain fabric

About 12 pieces of gold rick-rack, each 14 in. (35 cm) long

18 in. (45 cm) ribbon, ⅜ in. (1 cm) wide

8 x 2 in. (20 x 5 cm) colored felt for the crown

Polyester toy stuffing

Green and pink embroidery floss (thread)

White, gold, and green sewing thread

Paper

Pencil

Scissors

Pins

Sewing and embroidery needles

Pale pink felt-tip pen

1 Enlarge the templates on page 126 by 400%. Cut out a paper body and a paper mermaid tail.

2 Cut a strip of the spotty fabric measuring 2 x 12 in. (5 x 30 cm) and put it to one side. (This is for your mermaid's bikini top.) Fold the rest of the spotty fabric and the plain fabric or calico (muslin) in half. Pin the paper body to the plain fabric and the paper tail to the spotty fabric. Cut them both out so that you have two of each piece.

3 Using a pencil, mark on one of the fabric pieces for the body where the eyes and mouth will go; you can either copy the template or make your own face. Thread a needle with green embroidery floss (thread) and tie a knot in the end. Sew two French knots (see page 10) for eyes, starting and finishing on the back of the fabric.

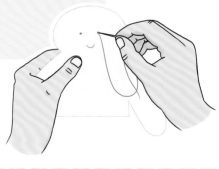

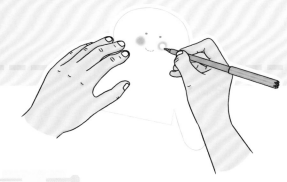

4 Now thread your needle with pink embroidery floss and tie a knot in the end. Starting and finishing on the back of the fabric, backstitch the mouth (see page 10). Draw two circles on the face using the pink felt-tip pen, so that your mermaid will have nice rosy cheeks.

5 Take one of the spotty tail pieces and lay it right side down on the embroidered piece, matching up the straight edges. Thread your needle with white sewing thread. Starting and finishing with a few small stitches, backstitch the two pieces together. Repeat this with the other spotty tail piece and the plain body piece to make the front and back of the mermaid.

6 Place the front of the mermaid onto the back of the mermaid, right sides together. Pin them together all the way around. Starting along one side of the mermaid and beginning with a few small stitches, backstitch almost all the way around; you should stop your stitches about 4 in. (10 cm) away from where you began to leave an opening. Finish with a few small stitches. Take out the pins.

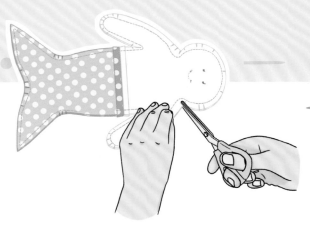

7 Where there's a deep curve in the mermaid shape—around the top of the head, under her arms, at the top of her fins and in the center of her tail—use sharp scissors to make small snips from the outside edge toward the stitches. Take care not to snip through the stitches! This will help to give your mermaid a nice shape.

8 Turn the mermaid right side out by carefully pulling the fabric through the opening. Push out the tail, arms, and head with the blunt end of a pencil. Take small pieces of stuffing and fill the mermaid, pushing the stuffing into the arms, legs, and head to make a nice round shape and making sure there are no lumps or bumps.

queen of the **MERMAIDS**

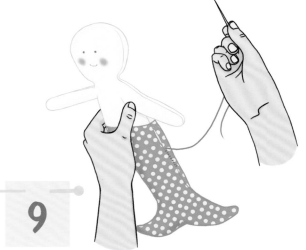

9 Where you left the opening in step 6, fold both edges of the fabric in until they're level with the stitched edge. Starting and finishing with a few small stitches to secure the thread, whipstitch the opening closed (see page 10).

10 Thread your needle with gold thread. To make the hair, stitch a few small stitches on the top of the head, then stitch through the middle of a piece of rick-rack and back through the top of the head. Sew all the pieces of rick-rack on like this, sewing each one a bit farther over the head. Finish with a few small stitches. The rick-rack will not cover the whole head, but the crown will hide where there's no hair.

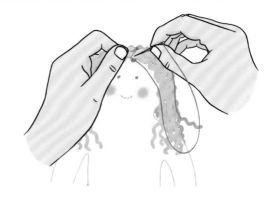

11 To make the bikini top, tie the middle of the ribbon around the middle of the fabric strip from step 2, then tie the ribbon around the mermaid's neck. Pass the ends of the fabric around under the mermaid's arms, positioning them to make a pretty bikini top. Pin them in place. Thread your needle with green thread and, starting with a few small stitches, stitch the bikini top together at the back, overlapping the ends. Then stitch through the bikini top onto the mermaid a few times to hold the top in place, and finish with more small stitches.

12 To make the crown, cut out a paper shape using the template on page 126, and cut the shape out of felt. Overlap the ends of the felt a little and sew a few running stitches along the overlap to join them together. Put the crown on your mermaid's head. You can stitch it in place, or leave it loose if you prefer.

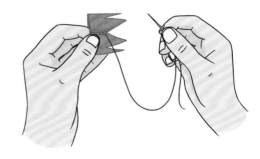

Sock Dog

Transform a stripy sock into a super-cute dog using your sewing skills and some embroidery floss! Choose a brightly colored sock (check with an adult first), look for two odd buttons and a few scraps of felt, then get to work. You can use this sock dog for inspiration or design your own creature with a funny face, maybe making your pup cross-eyed or giving it a big, funny nose.

You will need

Colorful, stripy long sock

Embroidery floss (thread) to match the sock

White and black embroidery floss

2-in. (5-cm) square of white felt

Scrap of black felt

2 odd buttons about ⅝ in. (15 mm) in diameter

Polyester toy stuffing

Ruler

Scissors

Pins

Embroidery needle

Paper and pencil

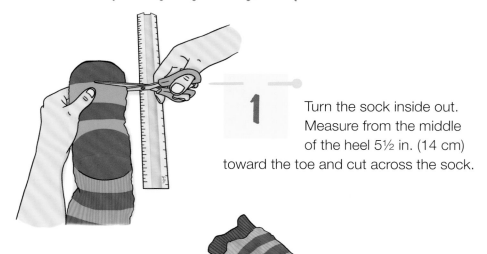

1 Turn the sock inside out. Measure from the middle of the heel 5½ in. (14 cm) toward the toe and cut across the sock.

2 Make a cut 1½ in. (4 cm) long down the middle of the sock from the cut edge.

3 Pin across and down the sides of both cuts. Tie a knot in the end of the matching embroidery floss. Using backstitch (see page 10), stitch along the cut edges to make two ears. Finish with a knot.

4 Turn the sock the right way out and push the ears out neatly. Measure 9½ in. (24 cm) down from the middle of the heel and cut across the sock, cutting off the ribbed cuff and setting it aside for later.

5 Push handfuls of toy stuffing inside the sock, making sure you fill the ears. Make the face (the heel) nice and round, and fill the body so that it looks plump.

6 Stop the stuffing before you reach the bottom edge. Cut a slit 2½ in. (6 cm) long in the middle of the bottom edge to make the legs. Turn the edges of the slit inside the sock. Tie a knot in the end of the matching embroidery floss and whipstitch the edges of the slit together (see page 10), leaving the bottom of each leg open. Don't cut the floss just yet.

7 Stuff the legs and finish whipstitching the first leg closed, turning in the edges as you stitch. Finish with a knot. Re-thread your needle and stitch the other leg closed.

8 To make the arms, use the cuff part of the sock that you cut off in step 4. This part was 3 in. (8 cm) long on the sock used here. Don't worry if yours is shorter—it just means that your dog's arms will be shorter! Lay the cuff flat and measure 1½ in. (4 cm) in from the edge. Cut down from here, in line with the ribbing on the cuff. Do the same on the other side, so that you have two arm pieces.

9 Open out one of the strips and then fold it the other way so that the wrong side is facing out. Pin along the long edge and the short ribbed end. Using matching floss, as before, backstitch along the pinned edges, starting and finishing with a knot.

10 Turn the arm the right way out and fill it with stuffing. Repeat steps 8–10 to make the second arm.

11 Turn the cut edge inside the arms a little and pin the arms to the body. Stitch them in place with a few running stitches.

12 To make the face, cut out a patch from white felt and a nose from black felt, using the photo on the left as a guide. Pin them onto the face and stitch them in place, using running stitches (see page 9) and embroidery floss to match the felt color.

13 Sew the buttons onto the face for eyes (see page 11). Tie a piece of embroidery floss around the neck to give the head more shape.

chapter 3
Stationery and Decorations

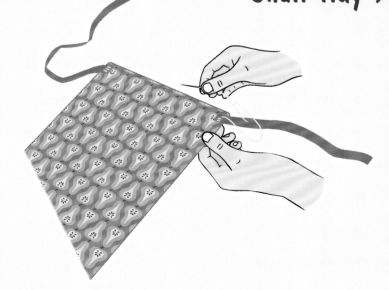

Bottle Bag

Whenever you go out for the day you always need a bottle of water—
and what better to carry it in than this bright over-the-shoulder
holder? You will need to use small, strong stitches... water is
heavy and you don't want your bag to fall apart!

You will need

10 x 12 in. (26 x 30 cm)
patterned fabric for the outside
of the bag

10 x 12 in. (26 x 30 cm)
gingham fabric for the inside
of the bag

White sewing thread

38 in. (96 cm) cotton tape,
¾ in. (2 cm) wide

Embroidery floss (thread) to
match the cotton tape

Scissors

Pins

Sewing and embroidery
needles

Pencil

Ruler

1 Fold the patterned fabric in
half along the long side with
right sides
together, so that it is 6 in.
(15 cm) wide. Pin down
one side and along the
bottom edge, leaving the top
edge open. Thread a sewing
needle with white sewing thread.
Starting and finishing with a few small
stitches, backstitch (see page 10) along
the pinned sides ⅜ in. (1 cm) from the edge.
Repeat with the gingham fabric—but this time
leave a gap of about 2 in. (5 cm) along the
bottom edge. Take out the pins.

2 Turn the patterned fabric right side out and gently
push out the corners. Push this bag inside the
gingham bag, so that the right sides of both bags
are together, with the seams together. Use your fingers inside
the bag to push the corners right into each other.

3

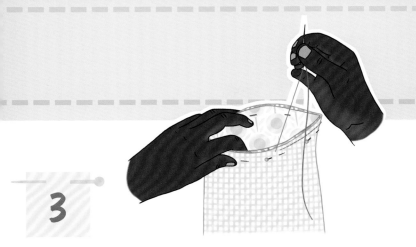

Pin the two fabrics together around the top edge of the bags. Using backstitch again, and starting and finishing with a few small stitches, sew the bags together all the way around the top. Take the pins out.

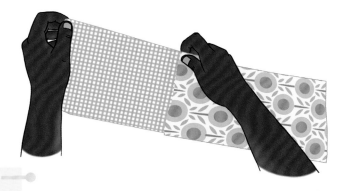

4 The next few steps are a bit fiddly, as there's lots of turning the bags inside out and then right side out again, but just take your time! Turn the whole bag right side out by pulling the bag through the gap in the stitching at the bottom of the gingham fabric. You will have a long tube. Pull out the corners neatly.

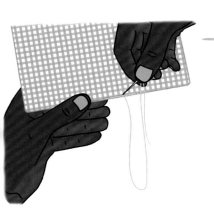

5 Where you left the gap in the gingham lining, fold both fabrics in until they're level with the stitched edge around the bottom edge of the bag. Starting and finishing with a few small stitches, whipstitch the gap closed (see page 10).

6 Push the lining inside the bag and push the corners out carefully with your fingers so that they look nice and neat.

bottle bag **77**

7 Turn the bag inside out so that the gingham fabric is on the outside and lay it flat on the table. Holding a corner between the fingers of each hand, push the corners together so that they make a point, then turn the bag so that the side seam in the fabric runs vertically down the bag to the point. You will have two pointy flaps on top of each other.

8 On the top flap, measure 1 in. (2.5 cm) from the point and draw a pencil line across. Starting and finishing with a few small stitches, make running stitches along the line, stitching through the top flap only. Turn the bag over and do the same on the other flap. This will make a nice, flat base for the bag.

9 Turn the bag right side out, so that the patterned fabric is on the outside. Fold the top edge over by ¾ in. (2 cm). Take the cotton tape and fold the ends under by ¾ in. (2 cm). Pin them to opposite sides of the bag, on the outside of the bag, with the ends a little lower than the folded-over edge. Thread your needle with embroidery floss (thread) and stitch the tape ends in place. Try to use small stitches, stitching in a square around the end of the tape to make sure the strap is strong. Start and finish with a knot.

Monster Pencil Case

Keep all your pens and pencils safe in this monster pencil case. Don't be put off by the zipper—it's actually really easy to add. Our monster has googly eyes and a cheeky pink tongue, but you could make up your own funny face or even turn your pencil case into an animal or an alien, using pieces of felt and buttons.

You will need

Templates on page 126

13 x 20 in. (35 x 50 cm) fabric—quite strong fabric is best

2 x 4 in. (5 x 10 cm) white felt

2 x 3 in. (5 x 8 cm) pink felt

Two black buttons

8-in. (20-cm) metal-toothed zipper

Needle and white thread

Pencil

Scissors

Pins

1 Enlarge the templates on page 126 by 200% and cut them out. Put the eyes and the tongue pieces to one side. Pin the pattern pieces to the fabric and cut them out so that you have one back piece, one top front piece, and one bottom front piece.

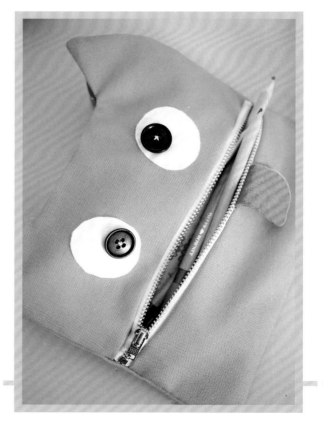

2 Fold the white felt in half and pin the paper pattern for the eyes to it. Pin the paper pattern for the tongue to the pink felt. Carefully cut out the pieces, then take out the pins and remove the patterns.

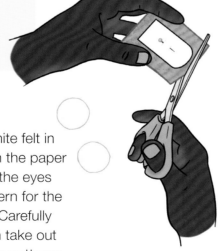

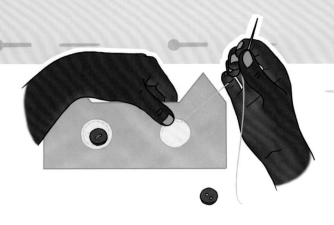

3 Pin the eyes onto the top front piece and stitch in place with running stitch (see page 9) starting and finishing with a few small stitches. Sew a button onto each felt eye, making them look a bit googly by positioning one higher than the other (see page 11 for how to sew on buttons).

4 Put the tongue about 2½ in. (6 cm) from the right-hand top corner of the bottom front piece and pin it in place.

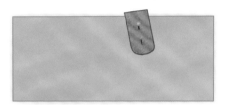

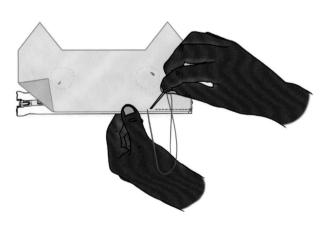

5 Put the zipper on the table, right side up. Place the top front piece on top of it, with the right side (the side with the eyes) facing down. Make sure the edge of the fabric is level with the edge of the zipper tape. Pin the fabric to the zipper tape. Using backstitch (see page 10), and starting and finishing with a few small stitches, stitch all the way along the top, ⅜ in. (1 cm) from the edge.

6 Flip the fabric over, so that the right side (with the eyes) is facing up. Place the bottom front on the zipper tape, again lining up the edges. Pin and stitch in the same way as before. Remove the pin from the tongue and open the zipper.

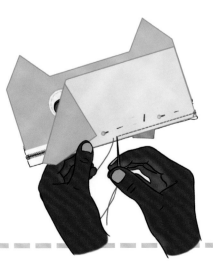

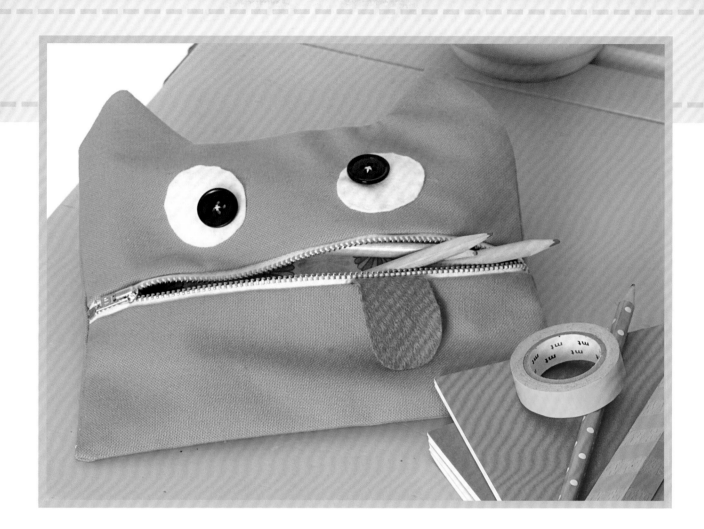

Make a pen-munching MONSTER

7 Lay the back piece on the table, with the right side facing up. Place the front panel on top of it, right side down. Match up all the edges and pin the pieces together. Using backstitch (see page 10), and starting and finishing with a few small stitches, stitch all the way along the top, ⅜ in. (1 cm) from the edge. Turn the pencil case right side out, pushing the corners and the ears out gently with your fingers.

Felt Stationery Pots ☺☺◯

Add a touch of style to your desk with these thick felt pencil pots (it's important to use thick felt, so that the pots are sturdy enough to stand up and hold their shape). Felt is sold in lots of fabric and craft stores and comes in great colors. The pots are really easy to make, so why not make several in different sizes to keep your jewelry and bits and bobs organized, too?

For each pot you will need

Template on page 126

12-in. (30-cm) square of thick felt

Thin white felt

White sewing thread

Yarn (wool) to match the felt

Ruler

Pencil

Scrap paper

Scissors

Pins

Sewing needle

Yarn (darning) needle

1 Using the ruler, draw a square measuring 4 x 4 in. (10 x 10 cm) on scrap paper and cut it out (see page 9). If you have some squared math paper, this will be easy. Cut three more squares the same as this one—be very accurate.

2 Photocopy the star template on page 126 or trace it onto scrap paper, and cut it out. Pin the paper star template to the thin white felt and cut it out neatly. Take off the pins and paper template.

3 Pin one paper square to each corner of the thick felt and cut along the two inner sides of each square so that all four corners of the felt have been cut off and you're left with a big cross shape. People who are good at math will recognize that it is the net of an open cube! Keep the bits of felt you've cut off to use in other projects.

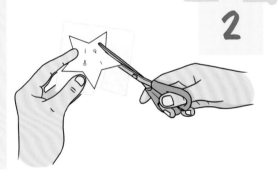

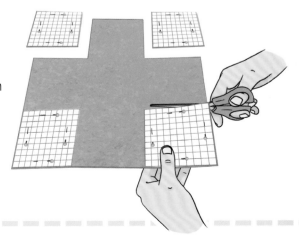

4

Pin the white felt star to the thick felt cross, making sure that it is in the middle of one of the outer squares of the cross. Thread your needle with white sewing thread. Using running stitch (see page 9), and starting and finishing with a few small stitches on the back of the felt, stitch the star in place.

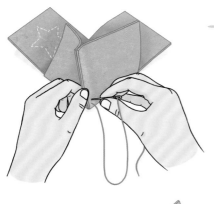

5

Thread a yarn (darning) needle with yarn (wool) and tie a knot in the end. Turn the felt over so that the star is facing downward. On one of the inside corners of the cross, push the needle through from the front to the back of the felt so that the knot is on top. Now fold up the two squares beside your needle to make two sides of the cube.

6

Pinch the edges of the felt together to make the corner of the cube. Starting at the bottom, push the needle through both layers of felt, and sew a running stitch (see page 9) close to the edge up to the top, pinching the edges together as you go. Finish with a knot on the inside of the cube. Trim the end of the yarn neatly.

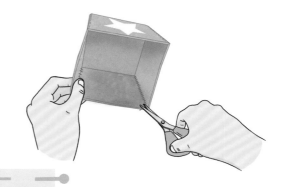

7

Stitch the three other corners in the same way. Trim the ends of the yarn so that they do not show.

Rick-rack Tote Bag

Stitch yourself a handy tote bag decorated with colorful rick-rack to carry your bits and bobs around. Most craft and haberdashery stores sell rick-rack in a wide range of widths and colors, but you could collect pieces of pretty ribbon and stitch those on instead if you prefer.

You will need

18 x 9 in. (46 x 23 cm) calico (muslin)

Lengths of rick-rack in bright colors at least 8 in. (20 cm) long

14 in. (35 cm) cotton tape, 1½ in. (4 cm) wide

White sewing thread

Tape measure

Paper

Pencil

Pinking shears

Scissors

Pins

Sewing needle

1 Measure and cut out a piece of paper 8 in. (20 cm) square (see page 9). Fold the calico (muslin) in half and pin the paper to it. Cut around the paper with pinking shears. (This will help to stop the fabric from fraying.) Take off the paper and pins. You will now have two squares of fabric.

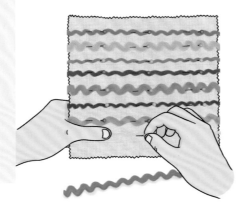

2 Take one of the squares and arrange the lengths of rick-rack across it. The first piece should be at least ¾ in. (2 cm) from the top of the square and the last one at least ¾ in. (2 cm) from the bottom to allow for the seams. Pin the rick-rack in place.

3 Using running stitch (see page 9), and starting and finishing with a few small stitches, sew across each piece of rick-rack. Take out the pins as you go.

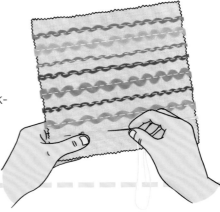

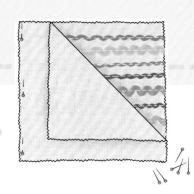

4

Put the decorated piece on the table, with the rick-rack facing upward. Put the other piece of fabric right side down on top. Pin the two layers together around the sides and bottom. Starting and finishing with a few small stitches, backstitch (see page 9) around the sides and bottom. The smaller and closer together your stitches are, the stronger the bag will be. Take out the pins as you go.

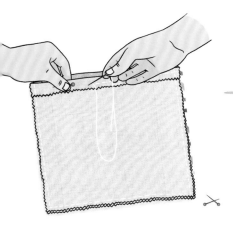

5

Turn the top edge over by ⅜ in. (1 cm) and pin in place. Starting and finishing with a few small stitches to secure the thread, sew running stitch all the way around to hem the top of the bag. Take out the pins as you stitch. Turn the bag right side out and gently push the corners out with your finger. Ask an adult to help you press the bag with an iron so that it's nice and flat.

6

Cut the cotton tape in half and fold the ends under by about ¾ in. (2 cm). Pin the ends of the tape to the top edge of the inside of the bag to make handles. Make sure all the handle ends are the same distance from the side seams. Starting and finishing with a few small stitches, sew the handles in place with backstitch, making the stitches as small as you can so that they will be nice and strong.

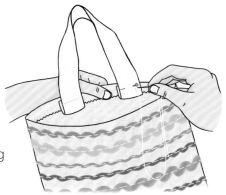

Cat Bookmarks

Never lose your page again with these cute cat-shaped bookmarks—the purr-fect gift for book-loving friends and family! Use thick, stiff ribbon if you can—grosgrain is ideal.

You will need

Templates on page 126

6 x 3 in. (15 x 8 cm) black, brown, or orange felt for the cat's head

1½ x 1 in. (4 x 2.5 cm) white felt for the stripe and button

Scrap of pink felt for the nose

5 x 2 in. (13 x 5 cm) colored felt for the shoes

10 in. (25 cm) grosgrain ribbon, 1½ in. (38 mm) wide

White sewing thread and sewing thread to match the head and shoes

White and black or brown embroidery floss (thread)

Paper

Pencil

Scissors

Pins

Sewing and embroidery needles

1 Photocopy the templates on page 126 or trace them onto scrap paper, and cut out a head shape, a stripe, a nose, shoes, and a button.

2 Fold the black, brown, or orange felt in half and pin the paper head to it. Cut it out neatly. Fold a small section of the white felt over and pin the paper button to it, then pin the paper stripe to the unfolded part of the white felt and cut out both pieces. Pin the paper nose to the pink felt and cut it out. Fold the colored felt for the shoes in half, pin the paper shoes to it, and cut them out. Then carefully cut out the inner sections on just one of the shoe pieces. (Small pointed scissors are best for this.)

3 Pin the white felt stripe to one of the head pieces, lining up the wider end of the stripe with the top of the head. Thread your needle with white sewing thread. Starting with a few small stitches on the back of the head, sew the stripe in place with running stitch (see page 9), adding the little pink nose at the bottom of the stripe, then finish with a few small stitches on the back of the head. Take out the pin.

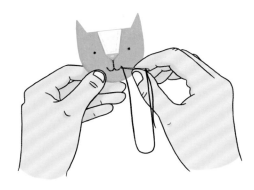

4 If you are making an orange or brown cat, cut a length of black embroidery floss (thread); if you are making a black cat, cut a length of brown floss. Tie a knot in the end. Thread your embroidery needle. Stitching from the back to the front, stitch two French knots (see page 10) on the face for the cat's eyes. Make a few backstitches (see page 10) to form the mouth, and finish with a knot on the back.

5 Thread the embroidery needle with white floss and tie a knot in the end. Working from the back of the head to the front, sew two stitches on either side of the nose to look like whiskers, finishing with a knot on the back.

6 Take the second head—the one without the cat's face—and put it on the table. Place the ribbon on it so that the top edge is just below the top of the head, and place the face on top of it. Pin them all together. Thread your sewing needle with thread to match the head. Starting and finishing with a few small stitches on the back, sew running stitch all the way around the face. Take out the pins.

7 Thread your embroidery needle with black floss and tie a knot in the end. Sew a white felt button onto each side of the front of the shoes (the bit that has the inner pieces cut out) by making two small stitches in a cross. Finish with a knot on the back of the shoes.

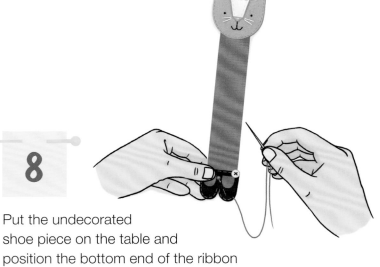

8

Put the undecorated shoe piece on the table and position the bottom end of the ribbon on it. Put the front of the shoes on the top, making sure the ribbon fills the cut-outs and you can't see its edges. Pin all the layers together. Thread your sewing needle with thread to match the shoes. Sew running stitch all the way around the shoes, starting and finishing with a few small stitches on the back of the shoes.

Mobile

This charming mobile is made from simple padded shapes stitched together from scraps of patterned fabric. We've tied the shapes onto a twig for a really pretty natural look, but you could fasten the cords to an embroidery hoop if you prefer.

You will need

Templates on page 125

10 x 8 in. (26 x 20 cm) fabric for the cloud

Two 14 x 7-in. (35 x 18-cm) pieces of fabric for the stars

10 x 6 in. (26 x 15 cm) fabric for the moon

Two 8 x 5-in. (20 x 13-cm) pieces of fabric for the raindrops

118 in. (300 cm) thin white cord

White sewing thread

Polyester toy stuffing

Twig about 24 in. (60 cm) long

Paper

Pencil

Scissors

Pins

Tape measure

Sewing needle

1 Enlarge the templates on page 125 by 400% and cut them out.

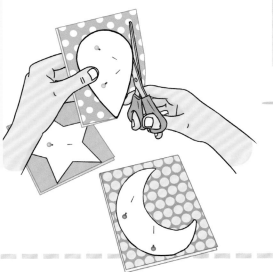

2 Fold all the pieces of fabric in half and pin a paper shape to each one. Carefully cut the shapes out, then take off the pins and paper.

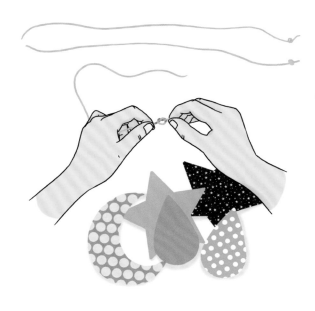

3 Cut six pieces of cord, each about 16 in. (40 cm) long. Tie a knot in the end of each one.

4 Place a knotted cord on the wrong side of a fabric shape, near the top of the shape, making sure the knotted end is on the fabric. Thread your needle with white sewing thread, then sew several stitches around the knot so that it is held firmly on the fabric.

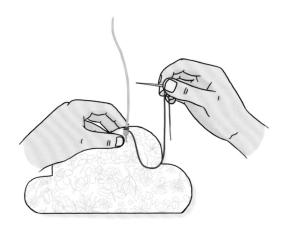

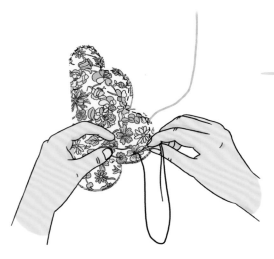

5 Take the fabric shape that matches the one you used in the previous step and put it on top of the first shape, right side up. Pin the two pieces together. Starting with a few small stitches to secure the thread, and using running stitch (see page 9), sew almost all the way around the two pieces, leaving a gap of about 1–2 in. (2.5–5 cm). Take the pins out—but don't cut the thread or pull the needle out, as you'll need them again.

6 Fill the shape with a few small bits of stuffing and then stitch the gap closed, finishing with a few small stitches again.

7 Make all the other shapes in the same way. Tie them onto the twig and hold in place with a knot. Make the shapes hang at different heights and trim the ends of the cords if necessary.

Bring the SKY inside

8 Tie the ends of the left-over piece of cord to the ends of the twig, then ask an adult to hang the mobile from the ceiling, balancing it so that it hangs level.

Star Pencil Toppers ●○○

These fun pencil toppers are really easy to make, so why not make lots of them in bright colors to liven up your pencil case? Decorate them with sequins or colorful beads, or leave them plain. Why not make some for your friends, too?

You will need

Templates on page 127

8 x 4 in. (20 x 10 cm) colored felt

Sequins

White sewing thread

Embroidery floss (thread) to match the felt

Paper

Pencil

Scissors

Pins

Sewing and embroidery needles

1 Photocopy the templates on page 127 or trace them onto scrap paper. Cut out a star shape and an inner shape.

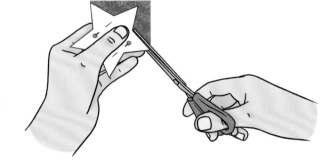

2 Fold the felt in half and pin the paper star to it. Cut out the felt stars as neatly as you can and take off the paper pattern.

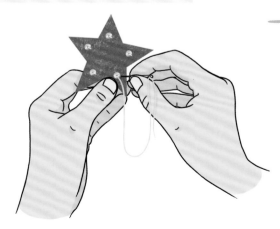

3 Thread your needle with white sewing thread. Make a few small stitches on the back of one star piece to secure the thread. Bring the needle from the back to the front of the star and carefully thread the needle through the hole in a sequin. Move the sequin down the thread so that it sits flat on the felt, and make a stitch across the sequin to its edge and back through the felt. You can sew the sequins on in a pattern or position them randomly—but don't put any where you will need to stitch in the next step. Finish with a few more small stitches.

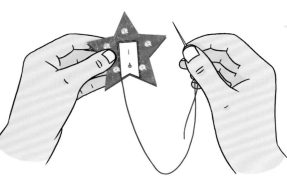

4 Pin the two felt stars together so that the sequined side is facing you, and pin the paper inner shape to the stars. Thread the embroidery needle with embroidery floss (thread) and tie a knot in the end. Working from the back of the star, sew running stitch (see page 9) around the paper inner shape, making sure you don't stitch through the paper. Don't stitch around the V-shaped point. Finish with a knot on the back of the star and take off the paper shape and pins. Push the pencil topper onto the end of a pencil.

Chair Tidy

Learn some sewing skills and keep your room tidy in one go with this handy project. Choose a fabric you like and stitch it together to make a pocket that ties onto the back of your chair for you to keep your bits and bobs in.

You will need

24 x 24 in. (60 x 60 cm) patterned cotton fabric

48 in. (120 cm) cotton tape or ribbon ½ in. (15 mm) wide

Pencil

Scissors

Pins

Needle and matching thread

Ruler

1 Fold the fabric in half with right sides together and pin around all three open sides. Thread your needle with thread to match the fabric. Starting and finishing with a few small stitches, backstitch around all three sides (see page 10). Stop stitching about 4 in. (10 cm) from the end to leave an opening. Take out the pins.

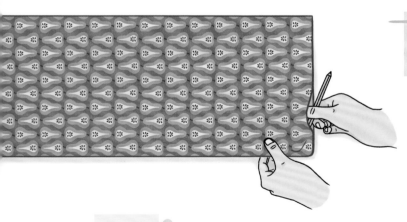

2 When you have finished sewing, turn the fabric the right way out by pulling it through the opening. Use the blunt end of a pencil to push the corners out and make them neat.

3 Where you left the opening in step 1, fold both edges of the fabric in until they're level with the stitched edge. Starting and finishing with a few small stitches to secure the thread, whipstitch the opening closed (see page 10).

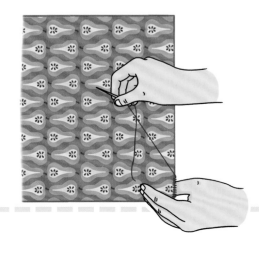

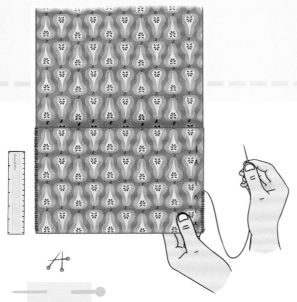

4 Lay the fabric on the table. Using the ruler, fold the bottom short edge up by 8 in. (20 cm). Pin the sides in place. Starting and finishing with a few small stitches, whipstitch along both sides to make the pocket. Take out the pins.

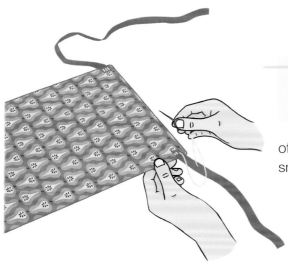

5 Cut the tape or ribbon into four 12-in. (30-cm) lengths. Fold one end of a piece of tape over by ½ in. (15 mm) and stitch it onto the wrong side of one of the corners of the chair tidy, on the other side from the pocket, making a few small backstitches to hold it firmly in place.

6 Do the same thing with the three remaining pieces of tape or ribbon so that all four corners have tape or ribbon attached. To use the chair tidy, lay the fabric over the back of your chair with the pocket facing outward, and tie the ribbons in neat, firm bows.

chapter 4
Gift Ideas

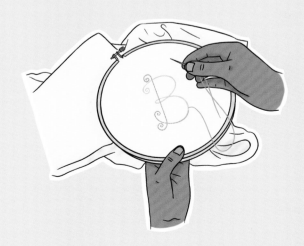

Cross-stitch Pillow

Why not make this cute little pillow for your room or to give as a gift? Gingham fabric is a great choice if you've never done cross stitch before, as you can stitch into the corners of the squares, which will guarantee that all your stitches are exactly the same size. You can make the pillow in any colors you like, but choosing a bright, contrasting thread will make your stitches really stand out.

You will need

Two 10½-in. (27-cm) squares of gingham fabric (the squares on the gingham measure ¼ in./7mm)

Embroidery needle and red embroidery floss (thread)

Sewing needle and white sewing thread

Polyester toy stuffing

Scissors

Air-soluble marker pen

Ruler

9-in. (23-cm) embroidery hoop

Pins

1 First you need to find the center white square of your fabric. To do this, fold one square of fabric in half to make a triangle, then fold it in half again to make a smaller triangle. The point of the right angle is the center. Use the marker pen to mark the nearest white square to this point with a small cross.

2 Undo the screw on the embroidery hoop and separate the outer and inner rings. Place the fabric over the inner ring. Fix the outer ring over it and tighten the screw, pulling the fabric tight as you go.

3 Following the photo above right, use the marker pen to mark the position of the crosses that make up the heart. You don't need to make a cross every time—a small dot is enough.

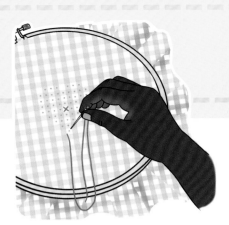

4

Thread the embroidery needle with red floss (thread) and tie a knot in the end. Bring the needle up from the back of the fabric to the front through the bottom left corner of the bottom marked square. Push the needle back down through the top right corner. You've made one diagonal stitch; this is the first half of the cross.

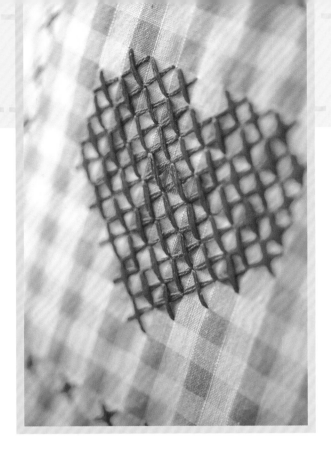

5

Bring the needle back up through the bottom right corner, and push it back down through the top left corner to make another diagonal stitch. Your first cross is complete!

6

To stitch the next line, bring your needle up through the bottom left corner of the first square in the row above. Now work from left to right and make a row of three diagonal stitches from bottom left to top right—one in each square. Then work back from right to left—so bring the needle up in the bottom right corner and take it down in the top left corner of each square in turn.

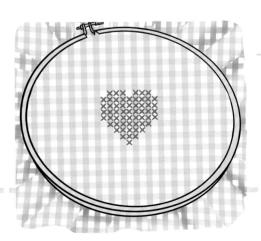

7

Stitch the next line in the same way, making five cross stitches this time. Carry on following your pen marks until the heart is complete. Finish with a knot or a few small stitches on the wrong side.

8 To mark out the crosses for the border, count down four squares from the bottom of the heart and make a pen mark in the fourth square. This should be a white square. Working outward from this square, mark every other square until you have marked four squares to each side of the first one. All the crosses for the border will be on white squares.

9 Working from left to right again, make a line of diagonal stitches going from bottom left to top right. Then work back the other way, from right to left, and make a line of stitches going from bottom right to top left.

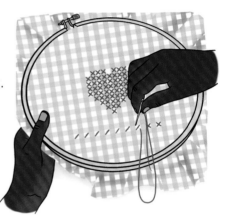

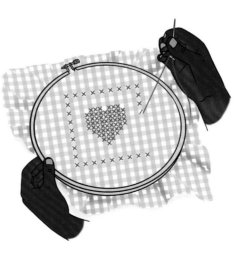

10 When you get back to where you started the border, miss the next square up, then stitch the square above (which will be white), stitching both diagonal stitches into a complete cross before you move up to the next one. From now on, the border is made with whole crosses stitched one at a time. Stitch seven more crosses so that the left side of the border is nine crosses high.

11 Make the border into a square by stitching another line of cross stitches across the top, then another one down the right-hand side in the same way. Finish with a knot on the wrong side of the fabric.

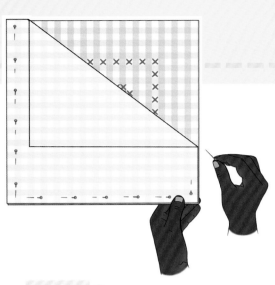

12 Take the fabric out of the hoop and ask an adult to help you press it gently with an iron on the reverse. Lay it right side up on the table (so you can see the crosses), place the other piece of fabric on top of it, and pin the two pieces together all the way around. Thread a sewing needle with white thread, and tie a knot in the end. Starting and finishing with a few small stitches, backstitch all the way around, leaving an opening of about 3 in. (8 cm) in one side. Take out the pins.

Cross your HEART!

13 Turn the cushion cover right side out and gently push out the corners. Fill the cover with stuffing, making sure it doesn't look lumpy. Where you left a gap in step 12, fold the edges of the fabric in so that they're level with the seam. Whipstitch the opening closed (see page 10), starting and finishing with a few small stitches.

Monogrammed Pillowcase

Personalize a pillowcase with a pretty embroidered initial.
Design your own letter or print one out using your computer and use
it as your pattern, stitching stars in pastel colors around it.

You will need

Plain pillowcase

8-in. (20-cm) embroidery hoop

Embroidery flosses (threads) in
7 different colors

Paper

Felt-tip pen

Scissors

Embroidery needle

Scissors

1 Undo the screw on the embroidery hoop and separate the inner and outer rings. Slide the inner hoop inside the pillowcase, into the corner where you want to stitch your monogram. Place the outer hoop over the fabric on top of the inner hoop and tighten the screw, gently pulling the fabric so that it is tight.

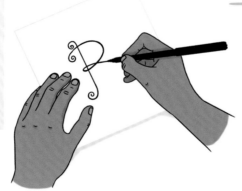

2 On paper, using a felt-tip pen, draw the letter you would like to embroider, making the lines thick. You could print out a really big (240-point) old-fashioned swirly capital letter from your computer if you are not sure how to draw a monogram letter.

3 Put the paper under the area of the pillowcase that you are going to embroider and trace the shape onto the pillowcase using the air-soluble marker pen.

Goodnight! SLEEP TIGHT!

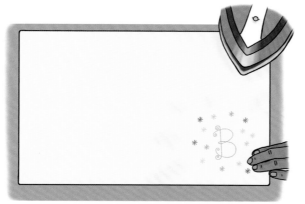

4 Thread the needle with a length of embroidery floss (thread) and tie a knot in the end. Put your hand inside the pillowcase, bring the needle up at the end of a line on your letter, and pull the floss so that the knot sits against the fabric. Sew neat backstitches (see page 10) along all the lines, finishing with a knot in the thread on the inside of the pillowcase.

Tip

Make sure you only stitch through the top layer of the pillowcase, otherwise you won't be able to open it to put the pillow inside!

5 Re-thread your needle with a different color of embroidery floss and tie a knot in the end. Put your hand inside the pillowcase, near the embroidered letter, and stitch a vertical stitch about ½ in. (12 mm) long. Push the needle back through the fabric and up again, and make another stitch horizontally across the first. Make two more straight stitches across these to make a star shape. Finish with a knot on the inside of the pillowcase, and trim the end of the floss.

6 Continue to sew stars around the embroidered letter, using different colors of floss. Sew the stars one at a time, starting and finishing with a knot on the underside, rather than stitching several stars at once, so that the threads on the inside will not show through to the front. Stitch about 15 stars or make your own design. Unscrew the hoop and take out the pillowcase. Ask an adult to help you press the pillowcase with an iron.

Key Rings

Everyone needs a key ring, and these jolly ones make a great gift. Choose your favorite colors—the brighter the better—and stitch them together using a co-ordinating button. Metal key rings are available from craft stores and online craft suppliers.

You will need

Templates on page 127

8 x 4 in. (20 x 10 cm) green or blue felt

3-in. (8-cm) square of pink or blue felt for the flower

2-in. (5-cm) square of dark pink or purple felt for the outer circle

1½ in. (4 cm) square of pale pink felt for the inner circle

Button, ½ in. (12 mm) in diameter

2 in. (5 cm) pink or blue ribbon

4-in. (10-cm) square of cardstock (cardboard) (an old cereal packet or similar)

White and green or blue sewing threads

Metal key ring

Paper

Pencil

Scissors

Pins

Sewing needle

1 Photocopy the templates on page 127 or trace them onto scrap paper, and cut out a large circle, a flower, and two smaller circles from paper. The large circle template should have a smaller circle drawn inside it; you'll need this later (see step 5).

2 Fold the largest piece of felt in half and pin the large paper circle to it. Cut it out neatly. Pin the paper flower shape to the pink or blue felt and the small paper circles to the purple or pink felt (you don't need to fold these pieces in half). Cut out all the shapes neatly.

3 Place the felt flower in the middle of one of the large circles of felt. Put the outer circle and then the inner circle on top. Pin through all the layers to keep them in place.

4 Thread your needle with white sewing thread. Start with a few small stitches on the back of the felt circle, then bring the needle up through the middle of the felt decorations pinned to the front. Stitch a few stitches through all the layers to hold them together, then take out the pin. Place the button in the middle of the flower, and this time stitch up through the felt and the button. Continue to stitch the button in place (see page 11), making sure you stitch through all the layers of felt. Then take the needle through to the back and finish with a few small stitches.

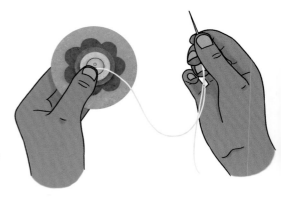

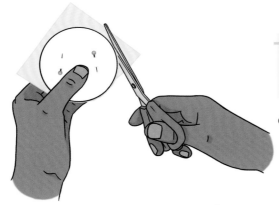

5 Cut out the smaller circle from the middle of the large circle template and draw around it on the cardstock (cardboard). Cut out the circle. This will be used to stiffen your key ring.

6 Take the second large circle of felt and put it on the table. Fold the ribbon in half and loop it through the metal keyring. Put the ends of the ribon on the felt circle so that about ½ in. (12 mm) of ribbon sticks out above the felt. Thread your needle with green or blue thread to match the felt, and stitch the ribbon to the felt with a few small stitches. Pull the needle out through the back, but leave it threaded.

7 Place the card circle on top of the piece with the ribbon, then place the front of the felt key ring on top of this and pin together around the edge, making sure you do not pin through the card.

Where are my KEYS...?

8 Using the threaded needle from step 6, sew running stitch (see page 9) around the outside of the felt, making sure you don't stitch through the card. Make your stitches very small and close together when you stitch through the ribbon, so that it's firmly held in place.

Bunting

This pretty bunting is simple to stitch and can be made with scraps of colorful fabrics left over from other sewing projects. It makes the perfect party decoration—or you could use it all year round to brighten up your bedroom. Cut out the fabric shapes using pinking shears so that the fabrics will not fray.

For a 90-in. (230-cm) length of bunting you will need

Template on page 127

9 pieces of fabric at least 9 in. (23 cm) square

90 in. (230 cm) cotton tape, ⅝ in. (15 mm) wide

White sewing thread

Paper

Pencil

Pins

Scissors

Pinking shears

Tape measure

Sewing needle

1 Enlarge the template on page 127 by 200% and cut it out. Pin the paper pattern onto each fabric in turn, then cut around it using pinking shears. (You can try to cut out two pieces at a time if you like, but if you find it easier to cut each one individually that's fine.) When you've cut each piece, take out the pins and remove the template.

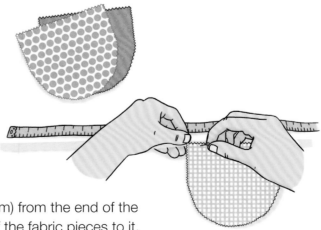

2 Measure about 10 in. (25 cm) from the end of the cotton tape, and pin one of the fabric pieces to it, lining up the edge of the fabric with the top edge of the tape. The wrong side of the fabric should be facing you.

Hang out the FLAGS!

3 Measure about 1 in. (2.5 cm) from the edge of the first piece of fabric (it doesn't need to be exact!) and pin another piece of fabric onto the tape. Repeat this until you've pinned on all nine pieces.

4 Starting with a few small stitches to secure the thread, sew running stitch (see page 9) along the top of the fabric and the tape, stitching right the way along the bunting. Take out the pins as you stitch. If you run out of thread, make a few small stitches to finish, then thread your needle with a new piece of thread and carry on in the same way, remembering to start with a few small stitches each time. Make sure you've taken out all the pins, then ask an adult to help you hang the bunting using the ends of the tape.

Cute Face Pillow

This cute pillow will make everyone smile! Simple appliqué is used to create a sweet face with a pretty ribbon bow stitched on to finish. Why not make one to look like a friend, using fabric in the same color as their hair and eyes to make the perfect personalized gift?

You will need

Templates on page 127

12½ x 25 in. (32 x 64 cm) calico (muslin) fabric

12½ x 8 in. (32 x 20 cm) brown spotty fabric

3 x 6 in. (8 x 15 cm) pink spotty fabric

2 x 3 in. (5 x 8 cm) brown felt

2-in. (5-cm) square of pink felt

12½ x 11 in. (32 x 28 cm) fusible bonding web

16 in. (40 cm) ribbon, 1½ in. (4 cm) wide

Black, pink, and white sewing threads

Polyester toy stuffing

Paper

Pencil

Scissors

Pins

Iron

Ironing board

Damp cloth

Sewing needle

1 Fold the calico (muslin) in half lengthwise and press it with your fingers to make a crease. Cut along the crease line to make two 12½-in. (32-cm) squares.

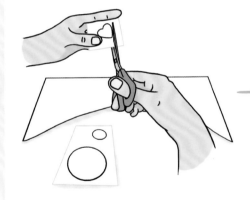

2 Enlarge the templates on page 127 by 400% and cut them out. Cut out paper patterns for the hair, an eye, a cheek, and the heart-shaped mouth.

3 Ask an adult to help you and, following the manufacturer's instructions, use an iron to attach fusible bonding web to the back of the pink and the brown spotty fabrics.

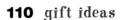

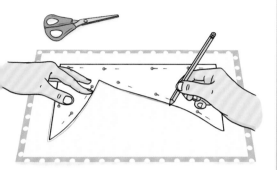

4 Turn the hair pattern over so that it's right side down, and pin it to the wrong side of the brown spotty fabric, on top of the fusible web. Draw around it. Take off the pattern and the pins, and cut out the hair shape.

A SWEET FACE for your bed

5 Peel off the backing paper from the fusible web on the brown spotty hair piece. Take one of the calico squares and place the hair piece along the top edge, matching up the corners. Place a damp cloth over the top and ask an adult to help you press it with a medium-hot iron. Check that the two fabrics have bonded together; if they haven't, replace the damp cloth and press for a little longer.

6 Fold the pink spotty fabric and the brown felt in half. Pin the paper pattern for the cheek to the spotty fabric, draw around it with a pencil, and cut it out carefully so that you have two pink cheeks. Now do the same thing with the brown felt and the paper eye pattern. Pin the paper mouth to the pink felt (you don't need to fold the felt in half this time) and cut it out. Take off the patterns and the pins.

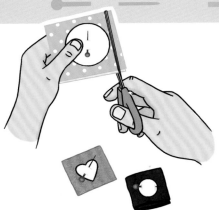

7 Now that you've cut out the eyes, cheeks, and mouth, place them on the pillow front underneath the hair piece and move them around until you're happy with the position. Then pin the eyes and mouth piece in place. You'll have to lift off the cheek pieces in the next step to peel off the backing paper, so before you do that make a few small marks around the top of each cheek piece with a pencil—then you'll know exactly where to put them back.

8 Peel the backing paper from each pink spotty cheek and place them on the cushion front on the line you drew earlier. Ask an adult to help you press them in place, using a damp cloth on top, in the same way as you pressed the hair piece in step 5.

9 Thread your needle with black sewing thread. Starting and finishing with a few small stitches on the back of the calico, sew a few running stitches (see page 9) around both eyes. Then thread your needle with pink sewing thread and sew on the mouth in the same way.

10 Put the second calico square on the front of the pillow and pin the two layers together all the way around the edge. Thread your needle with white sewing thread. Starting and finishing with a few small stitches, backstitch (see page 10) almost all the way around, leaving a gap in the stitching of about 4 in. (10 cm).

11 Turn the cover right side out through the gap and push the corners out so that the cover is nice and square. Fill the cover with stuffing, then whipstitch (see page 10) the gap closed, starting and finishing with a few small stitches.

12 Tie the ribbon in a neat bow. Using a needle and pink thread, make a few small stitches in the pillow where the hair meets the face. Stitch the bow firmly onto the cover and finish with a few more small stitches.

Bandana Apron

Protect your clothes when you're baking by wearing this colorful apron made from a store-bought bandana. It would also make a great gift for a friend who loves to cook. Bandanas come in a huge range of colors, but if you can't find one you could use a square of fabric instead and sew a running stitch all around the edge to hem it.

You will need

Bandana (square headscarf)—this one is 21 in. (53 cm) square

80 in. (2 m) cotton tape or ribbon, ½ in. (12 mm) wide

Ruler

Pinking shears or scissors

Needle

Sewing thread to match the bandana

White sewing thread

Pins

Safety pin

1 Lay the bandana on a flat surface or a table with one of the corners pointing up. Fold the top corner down by 6 in. (15 cm) and press along the fold with your fingers to make a crease. This makes a triangle. Use your ruler to check that the two sides are the same length.

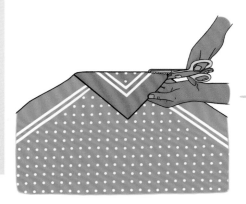

2 Cut along the crease with pinking shears if you have them. (Ordinary scissors will work just as well, but the fabric may fray a little.)

3 Fold the edge that you have just cut over to the wrong side (the back of the fabric) by ¾ in. (2 cm). Thread a needle with sewing thread that matches the bandana. Starting and finishing with a few small stitches, sew the fold in place with running stitch (see page 9), stitching ¼ in. (6 mm) from the cut edge.

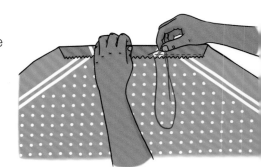

4

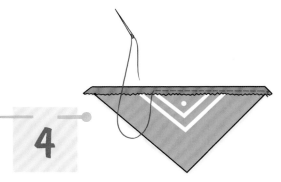

Take the top corner that you cut off in step 2 and fold the cut edge over to the wrong side by ⅜ in. (1 cm). Sew running stitch all the way along this edge, starting and finishing with a few small stitches.

5 Fold the corners over to the wrong side by 1¾ in. (4.5 cm) and press along the fold with your fingers to form a crease. Now you have a neat pocket shape.

6 Lay the bandana on a table, with the stitched edge at the top. Place the pocket on the bandana so that the bottom point of the pocket is 11 in. (28 cm) from the bottom point of the bandana and the same distance from either side. Measure it with your ruler! Pin the pocket in place, leaving the top edge open.

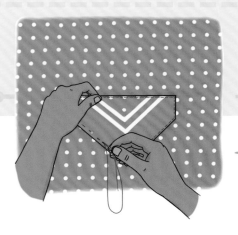

7 Starting and finishing with a few small stitches, sew the pocket in place with running stitch. Don't sew along the top edge! When you've finished, take out all the pins.

8 Cut a length of cotton tape or ribbon about 45 in. (115 cm) long to tie around your neck, and fasten the safety pin to one end of it. Push the safety pin through the stitched channel on the top of the bandana until it comes out of the other side. Pull the tape through until you have the same amount sticking out of each side of the channel, then take off the safety pin.

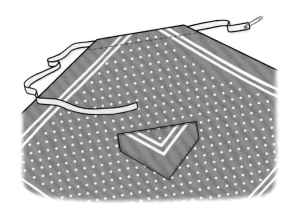

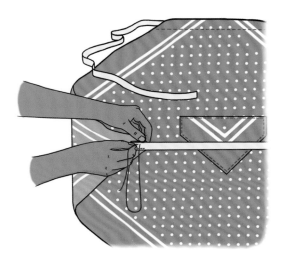

9 Now make the waist ties. Cut the rest of the tape or ribbon in half. Fold the end of one piece over by ⅝ in. (1.5 cm) and pin it to a side corner of the bandana. Thread your needle with orange sewing thread. Starting and finishing with a few small stitches on the back, backstitch (see page 10) the tie in place, making the stitches quite small so that they will be strong. Stitch the other piece of tape to the other side corner in the same way.

10 Try the apron on!

Envelope Bag

Envelope bags are all the rage—but rather than spend a lot of money buying one, why not make one instead? To make it into a purse, simply stitch a length of ribbon onto it for a handle, checking that it is long enough before you sew it in place.

You will need

12½-in. (32-cm) square each of two co-ordinating fabrics

Scrap cardstock (cardboard) 7½ in. (19 cm) square—you could use an empty cereal packet

1 popper snap (press stud)

Self-cover button, 1¼ in. (3 cm) in diameter

Matching sewing thread

Pins

Sewing needle

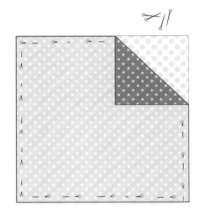

1 Put one of the squares of fabric right side up on the table and place the second piece right side down on top. Match up all the sides and pin the two layers together all the way around.

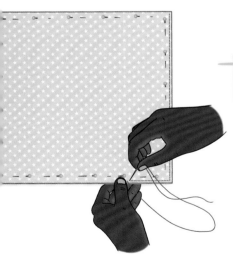

2 Thread your needle with sewing thread to match the fabric. Starting and finishing with a few small stitches, backstitch (see page 10) almost all the way around, leaving an opening of about 4 in. (10 cm) at the end. Don't cut the thread—you'll need it again later.

3 Take out the pins, then turn the bag right side out by carefully pulling the fabric through the opening in the stitching. Push the corners out carefully with the blunt end of a pencil to make them neat.

4 Where you left the opening in step 2, fold both edges of the fabric in until they're level with the stitched edge. Starting and finishing with a few small stitches, whipstitch (see page 10) the opening closed. Ask an adult to help you press the bag with an iron.

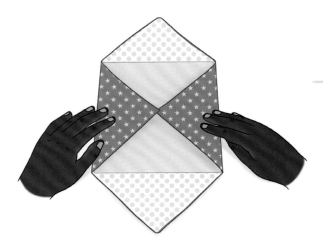

5 Put the fabric square on the table with the corners at the top and bottom, like a diamond. The fabric that you want to be on the inside of the bag should be facing upward. Put the cardstock (cardboard) square on top of it so that it is square to you. Fold the sides in so that the points meet in the middle.

6 Fold the bottom corner up so that it overlaps the side flaps a tiny bit and the point is just above | where the two side points meet. Pin the three flaps together, making sure you do not pin through the card.

7 Starting and finishing with a few small stitches on the wrong side to secure the thread, neatly backstitch along both sides of the bottom flap to join it to the side flaps. The card will stop you from stitching through the back of the fabric—but make sure you don't stitch through the card! Ask an adult to help you press the bag again, so that it's nice and flat.

8 Separate the two parts of the popper snap (press stud). Thread your needle and stitch a few small stitches onto the bottom flap, just below the tip. Then sew one part of the popper snap over these, bringing your needle up through each of the holes, around the edge of the popper, and back down through the fabric two or three times. Finish with a few more small stitches to secure the thread firmly. Now take the card out. Fold down the top flap. With your pencil, mark the place on the inside that meets the popper on the bottom flap. Sew the second part of the popper snap where you have made the mark.

SMART and SOPHISTICATED!

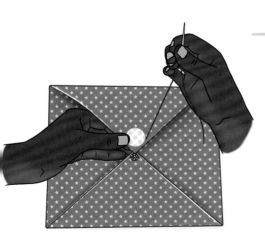

9 On the packet of self-cover buttons, there will be a template for the size of button that you are using. Cut this out, draw around it on a scrap piece of fabric, then cut out the fabric circle. Following the button manufacturer's instructions, separate the button into its two pieces. Place the button front on the back of the fabric circle, making sure it fits neatly. Fold the fabric around the button, stretching it tight and pushing it down over the teeth on the back. Press on the button back so that the two halves snap together. Stitch the button onto the tip of the top flap, on top of the popper (see page 11). Again, with the help of an adult, press the bag one last time—this will finish it beautifully.

Doll's Blanket

Give your doll or teddy this cozy woolen blanket to keep them warm. It's decorated with appliquéd circles and has blanket stitches all the way around, so it looks really pretty. Blanket stitch is easy to do, but it takes a little practice—so try it out on some scrap fabric first, so that you get the hang of it before you start on the actual blanket.

You will need

24 x 18 in. (60 x 45 cm) cream wool or fleece fabric

3-in (8-cm) squares of six different-colored felts

Green yarn (wool)

Sewing threads to match the colored felts

Scissors

Pins

Yarn (darning) and sewing needles

Small cups to draw around

Paper

Pencil

1 To edge the blanket, take the wool or fleece fabric, turn ⅜ in. (1 cm) to the wrong side along one edge, and pin the edge in place.

2 Thread a yarn (darning) needle with green yarn (wool) and tie a knot in the end. Starting near one corner, blanket stitch (see page 11) along the folded edge all the way to the next corner. When you've finished this edge, take out the pins.

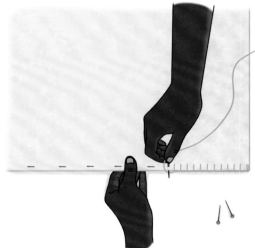

3 Turn the blanket around and repeat steps 1 and 2 along the next side, again pinning the folded edge down and blanket stitching along. Work one side at a time so that you will not have too many pins in your fabric while you sew. Do this until you have stitched around all four sides. Finish with a knot on the back of the blanket.

4

Find two small, round cups to draw around—one that measures about 2 in. (5 cm) across and a smaller one about 1½ in. (4 cm) across. Draw around them on paper and cut out the circles to use as templates.

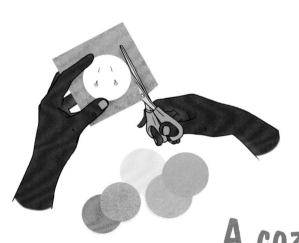

A cozy, COMFORTING blanket

5

Pin the circles to the squares of colored felt and cut out three large felt circles and three small felt circles—all in different colors.

6

Arrange the circles on one corner of the blanket and pin them in place. Using sewing thread to match the felt, stitch the felt circles in place with small straight stitches, starting each one with a few small stitches on the back of the blanket. As you finish each circle, take out the pins.

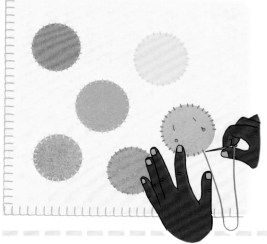

Templates

For instructions on how to use these templates to make patterns, see page 8. Most of the templates on these pages are printed at half size and a few are quarter size—all of them are labeled so you know by how much they need to be enlarged. Templates printed at actual size do not need to be enlarged.

Raccoon scarf: half size, enlarge by 200%

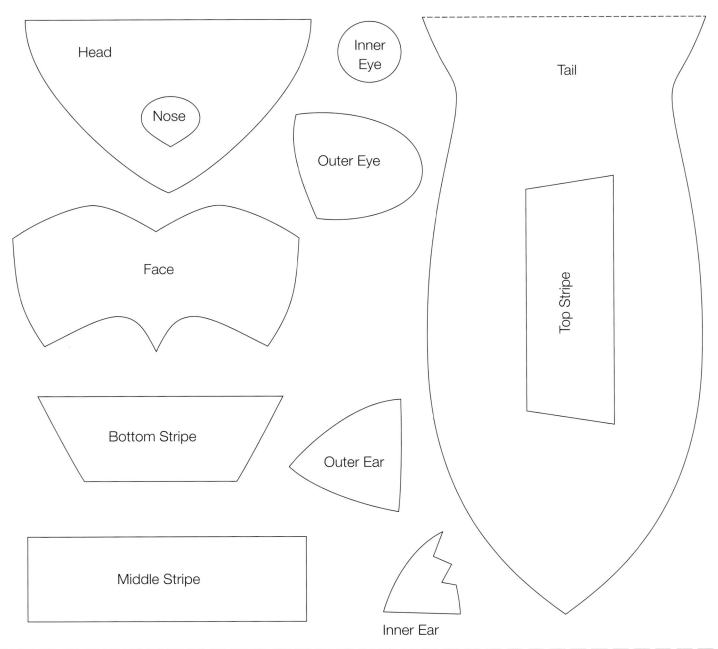

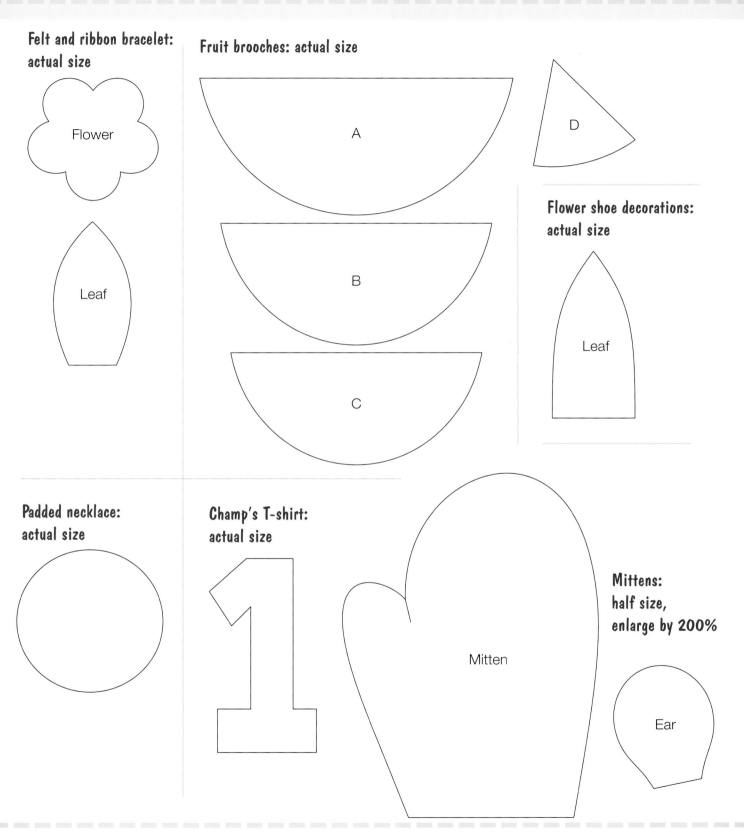

Felt and ribbon bracelet: actual size

Flower

Leaf

Fruit brooches: actual size

A

B

C

D

Flower shoe decorations: actual size

Leaf

Padded necklace: actual size

Champ's T-shirt: actual size

Mitten

Mittens: half size, enlarge by 200%

Ear

Felt mice: half size, enlarge by 200%

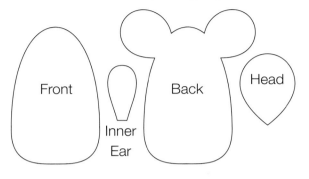

Felt bugs: half size, enlarge by 200%

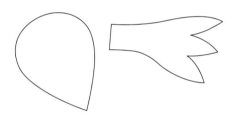

Felt vegetables—radish: half size, enlarge by 200%

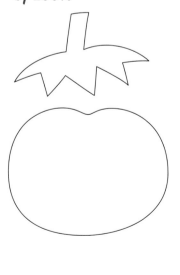

tomato: half size, enlarge by 200%

eggplant (aubergine): half size, enlarge by 200%

carrot: half size, enlarge by 200%

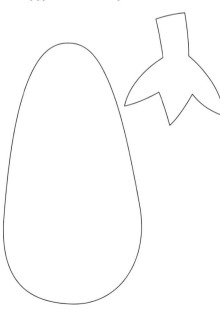

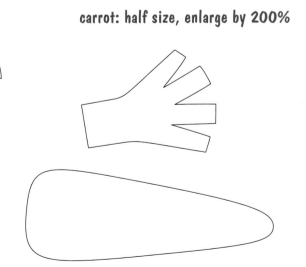

Felt vegetables—lettuce: half size, enlarge by 200%

Teddy bear: half size, enlarge by 200%

Dog finger puppets: half size, enlarge by 200%

Body

Ear

Ear

Ear

Snout

Head

Nose

Pom-pom

Eye patch

Mobile: quarter size, enlarge by 400%

Raindrop

Moon

Cloud

Star

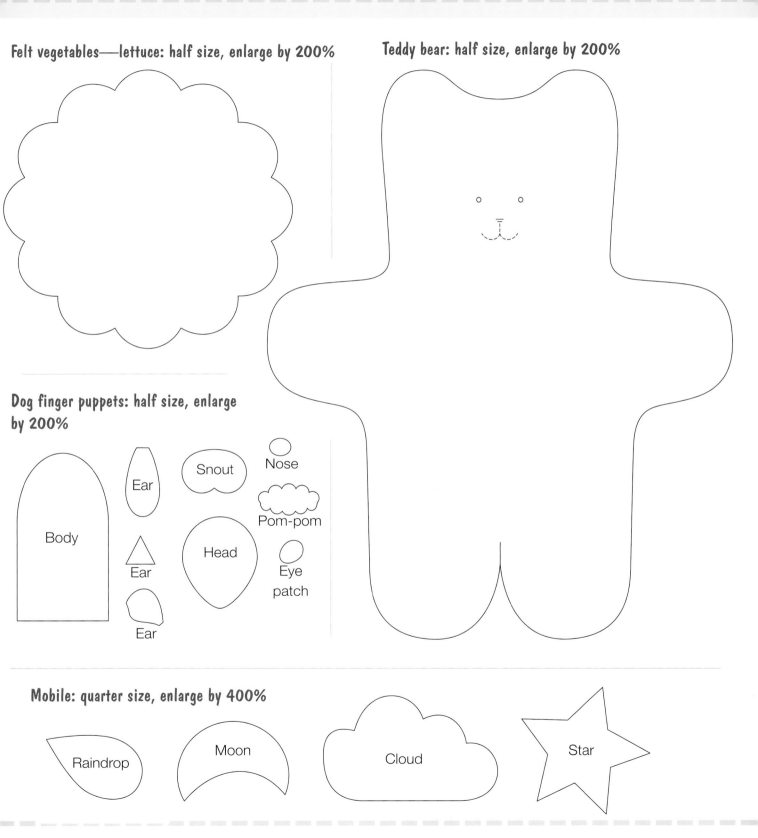

Mermaid: quarter size, enlarge by 400%

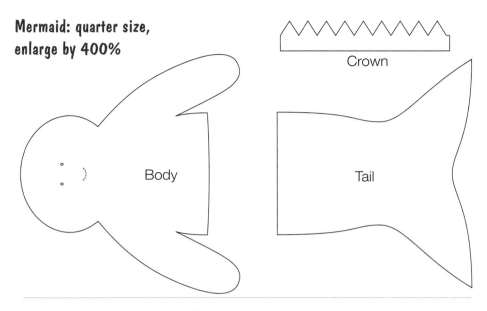

Crown

Body

Tail

Cat bookmarks: actual size

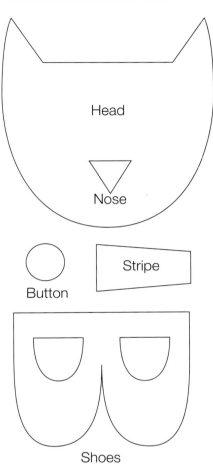

Head

Nose

Button

Stripe

Shoes

Monster pencil case: half size, enlarge by 200%

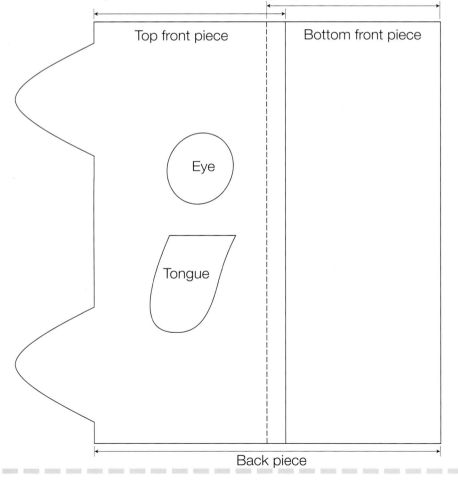

Top front piece

Bottom front piece

Eye

Tongue

Back piece

Felt stationery pots: actual size

Star pencil toppers: actual size

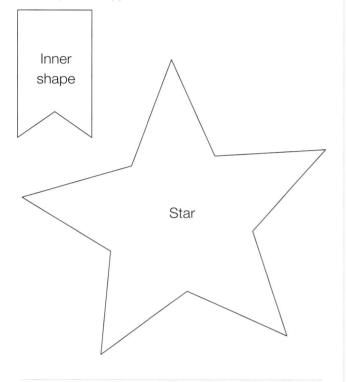

Inner shape

Star

Bunting: half size, enlarge by 200%

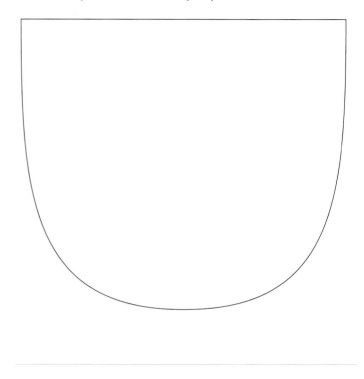

Cute face pillow: quarter size, enlarge by 400%

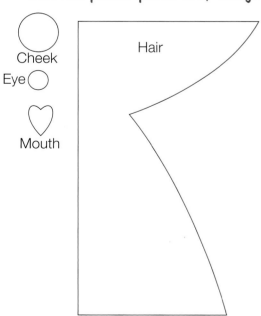

Cheek

Eye

Mouth

Hair

Key rings: actual size

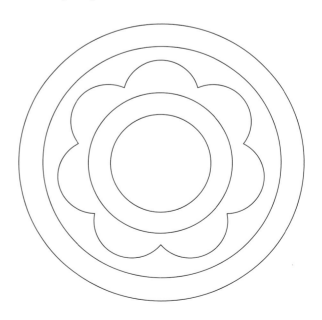

Index

Suppliers

US
Create For Less
www.createforless.com

Hobby Lobby
www.hobbylobby.com

Jo-ann Fabric & Crafts
www.joann.com

Michaels
www.michaels.com

UK
Buttonbag
www.buttonbag.co.uk

Hobbycraft
www.hobbycraft.co.uk

John Lewis
www.johnlewis.com

Acknowledgments

Thank you to Debbie Patterson
for photographing the book so
beautifully and for always finding
the perfect spot for each project.
Thank you to Sarah Hoggett who,
as ever, remained calm and
supportive throughout the editing
process, to Susan Akass for
checking it all so well, to Rachel
Boulton for understanding and
illustrating each project, and to
Barbara Zuniga for the design of the
book. Thank you to Kerry Lewis for
finding and booking lovely locations
and to Anna Galkina for overseeing
and supporting the book so well
from start to finish. Thank you also
to Cindy Richards who trusted me
(again!) and gave me the opportunity
to do another book for CICO and to
work with such lovely people. Thank
you all so much.